T3-BAI-188

JONAS SALK SCHOOL
2950 HURLEY WAY
SACRAMENTO, CA 95864

D0623249

Basic Domestic Pet Library

Hamsters Today
A Complete and Up-to-Date Guide

Dennis Kelsey-Wood

Published in association with T.F.H. Publications, Inc.,
the world's largest and most respected publisher of pet literature

Chelsea House Publishers
Philadelphia

<u>Basic Domestic Pet Library</u>
A Cat in the Family
Amphibians Today
Aquarium Beautiful
Choosing the Perfect Cat
Dog Obedience Training
Dogs: Selecting the Best Dog for You
Ferrets Today
Guppies Today
Hamsters Today
Housebreaking and Training Puppies
Iguanas in Your Home
Kingsnakes & Milk Snakes
Kittens Today
Lovebirds Today
Parakeets Today
Pot-bellied Pigs
Rabbits Today
Turtles Today

Publisher's Note: All of the photographs in this book have been coated with FOTO-GLAZE®
finish, a special lamination that imparts a new dimension of colorful gloss to the photographs.

Reinforced Library Binding & Super-Highest Quality Boards

This edition © T.F.H. Publications, Inc., 1 TFH Plaza, Neptune City, NJ 07753. This special
library bound edition is made expressly for Chelsea House Publishers, a division of Main Line
Book Company.

1 3 5 7 9 8 6 4 2

Library of Congress Cataloging-in-Publication Data

Kelsey-Wood, Dennis & Eve.
     Hamsters today: a complete and up-to-date guide / Dennis Kelsey-Wood.
          p. cm. -- (Basic domestic pet library)
     "Approved by the ASPCA"
     Includes index.
     ISBN 0-7910-4609-5 (hardcover)
1. Hamsters as pets.
I. American Society for the Prevention of Cruelty to Animals.
II. Title. III. Series.
SF459.H3K44 1997
636.9'356--dc21

97-4192
CIP

HAMSTERS TODAY

yearBOOKS, INC.
Glen S. Axelrod
Chief Executive Officer

Mark Johnson
*Vice President Sales
& Marketing*
Barry Duke
Chief Operating Officer

Neil Pronek
Katherine J. Carlon
Managing Editors

DIGITAL PRE-PRESS
Ken Pecca
Supervisor

John Palmer
Jose Reyes
Digital Pre-Press Production

Computer Art
Patti Escabi
Candida Moreira
Michele Newcomer

Advertising Sales
Nancy S. Rivadeneira
Advertising Sales Director
Chris O'Brien
Advertising Account Manager
Jennifer Johnson
Advertising Coordinator
Adrienne Rescinio
*Advertising Production
Coordinator*
c yearBOOKS, Inc.
1 TFH Plaza
Neptune City, NJ 07753
**Completely Manufactured in
Neptune City, NJ USA**

Anmarie Barrie

Although the golden hamster was identified over 150 years ago, it was not until the 1950s that it started to gain fame and popularity as a domestic pet. Today, the hamster, in its many colors, patterns and coat varieties, is arguably the most loved of the small rodents kept by children as a pet. Unlike its rodent contemporaries—rats, mice and gerbils—the hamster has only the remnants of a tail. This feature has endeared it to the moms of the world, who do not view it as a creature of terror, or the spreader of disease. Its image has remained untarnished, a fact that cannot be said of rats and mice in particular.

The hamster is a small cuddly little critter with a cute facial expression and a very inquisitive nature. It is best kept as a single pet—just one of its many virtues that make it an excellent choice for children. It is inexpensive, even a high-quality individual not being costly. As a subject for exhibition and breeding, it is no less an excellent choice for the older child and for adults. The many colors and coat patterns provide more than sufficient challenge to the discerning hobbyist. The availability of other hamster species in recent years has created fresh impetus for hamsters as a group.

One way or the other, the future for this fascinating little pet is very good. It can certainly be well recommended as a pet: a whole hobby industry has been specifically built up around it, so you can both care for it and enjoy its many appealing attributes.

In the following chapters, everything you need to know about the hamster is discussed. Whether you simply want one or two pets, or wish to breed and exhibit, the subjects are explained in sufficient detail that nothing of importance is omitted. The superb color photographs provide a fine representative selection of the numerous varieties. From them, you can determine which kind of hamster you would like to begin with.

© **by T.F.H. Publications, Inc.**
Distributed in the UNITED STATES to the Pet Trade by T.F.H. Publications, Inc., One T.F.H. Plaza, Neptune City, NJ 07753; on the Internet at www.tfh.com; in CANADA Rolf C. Hagen Inc., 3225 Sartelon St. Laurent-Montreal Quebec H4R 1E8; Pet Trade by H & L Pet Supplies Inc., 27 Kingston Crescent, Kitchener, Ontario N2B 2T6; in ENGLAND by T.F.H. Publications, PO Box 15, Waterlooville PO7 6BQ; in AUSTRALIA AND THE SOUTH PACIFIC by T.F.H. (Australia), Pty. Ltd., Box 149, Brookvale 2100 N.S.W., Australia; in NEW ZEALAND by Brooklands Aquarium Ltd. 5 McGiven Drive, New Plymouth, RD1 New Zealand; in SOUTH AFRICA, Rolf C. Hagen S.A. (PTY.) LTD. P.O. Box 201199, Durban North 4016, South Africa; in Japan by T.F.H. Publications, Japan—Jiro Tsuda, 10-12-3 Ohjidai, Sakura, Chiba 285, Japan. Published by T.F.H. Publications, Inc.

MANUFACTURED IN THE
UNITED STATES OF AMERICA
BY T.F.H. PUBLICATIONS, INC.

CONTENTS

*A cinnamon satin female hamster
enjoying a snack of fresh greens.*

Golden satin and satin longhaired female hamsters.

A golden hamster. This variety has been a popular pet since the 1950s.

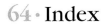

Fancy hamster varieties do not resemble the original Golden, or Syrian, hamster either in color or personality. Wild hamsters are not good pets. Your local pet shop can show you many color varieties.

WHAT IS A HAMSTER?

Hamsters are members of that group of animals known as rodents. These mammals, when viewed in terms of number of species, are the most successful mammals on earth at this time. Within the kingdom Mammalia there are about 4,500 species. The order Rodentia contains 1,814 of them (40 percent). Only the 986 species of bats (order

cavies, porcupines, and of course gerbils and hamsters.

The success of the order stems from their ability to adapt to a wide range of climatic and environmental conditions, to survive on an equally wide range of foods, to breed readily, to their small size and, in many instances, to their nocturnal habits. From a economic viewpoint, certain

parts of its range. This is no longer the case.

RODENT FEATURES

The most noticeable feature of rodents is their teeth, the incisors of which are especially adapted for gnawing. In other features, rodents are quite variable. Some have long furred tails; others have naked tails. Hamsters, along with many other rodents, have only a small tail. Ear size ranges from very small to unusually large—as in species adapted for desert life. Rodents may have very

The term **hamster,** *like the word* **squirrel,** *refers to storing food. This hamster has its mouth filled with food which it will hide someplace, to be devoured later when it is hungry.*

Chiroptera) come anywhere close to the number of rodent species.

Most rodents are small; but the largest member of the order, the South American capybara, which looks something like a giant guinea pig, can weigh as much as 170 lbs. Rodents are found almost world wide, living underground, on the surface, or in trees. Being such a large order, there are many group members that are familiar to you—rats, mice, squirrels, beavers, lemmings, chinchillas,

rodents, such as rats and mice, have gained a notorious reputation as being both carriers of disease, as well as consumers of millions of tons of grain and other foods each year. The cost of controlling rodent populations runs into billions of dollars every year. However, the vast majority of rodent species represent no threat to humans, avoiding them as much as possible. Hamsters are among these rodent species, though some years ago the common hamster was regarded as a pest in many

long hind limbs that enable them to move about by hopping, or they may have folds of skin that enable them to glide. But most move around by running, often at high speed relative to their size.

All rodents are able to use their front feet much like hands. The elbow joint is quite flexible to allow a wide range of movement. There are normally five digits on the front feet and three to five on the rear legs. A number of rodents, which includes most hamsters, have cheek pouches in which food can be carried to be eaten where it is more safe, or stored for consumption when times are hard. The latter caches of food can at times be considerable. The cheek pouches of the hamster are very large when packed with seeds and other edibles. Many rodents, again including the hamster, will hibernate during periods of adverse weather, but become active for short periods. During these periods, they will feed on their stored foods. The intestinal tract of rodents will reflect their type of nutrition. In some, the stomach is very short, suggesting a diet essentially of insects or small animals. In others, it is more complex, being even ruminant-like in some instances. This indicates a very herbivorous diet—plant matter needing a greater period in the stomach to be digested than does food of animal origin. The hamster is capable of digesting foods of both types. It

Hamsters are rodents and must have something upon which to chew so they can keep their sharp incisor teeth worn down.

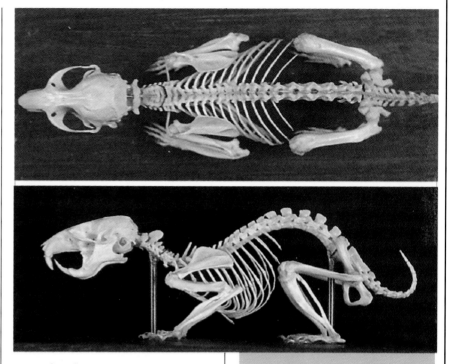

is said to be an omnivorous feeder, but with a strong leaning toward being herbivorous.

RODENT DENTITION

Given the special importance of teeth to the hamster, and all other rodents, pet owners should understand their basic structure, particularly the incisors. Failure to do so can result in a pet having all kinds of problems. The teeth grow continually throughout the life of the hamster. The incisors have open roots and are shaped rather like a chisel, the outer part being higher than the inner part, thus creating a chisel-like angle. The outer part is also harder than the inner part. This helps the process of self sharpening as the teeth rub against each other, and against hard foods.

The incisors of the upper jaw overlap, but just touch, those of the lower jaw. Any other arrangement would mean that the teeth could not wear down as they should. The result is

The skeletons of a hamster shown in both top view and side view show how powerful their jawbones are and how large are their incisor teeth.

that they would grow up or down as the case may be. They could penetrate the roof or base of the opposite jaw. This would mean the hamster could not eat its food and would starve. There is some capacity to overcome minor misalignment, as the lower jaw is quite mobile, and can be moved sideways and forward.

The condition created by misalignment is called malocclusion and is caused by one of three reasons:

1. It may be genetic, in which case such an individual must never be used for breeding, no matter how outstanding it may be in all other features. The genetic base itself may be directly related to the teeth, or to the

skull as a whole. If breeders select and breed for a longer or shorter head, this will of course affect jaw size, thus altering the relationship of one jaw to the other.

2. It may be caused by the pet habitually biting on the cage bars. In so doing, it can alter the direction of the teeth enough to cause misalignment.

3. It may be caused by the hamster's having inadequate

There are no suitable hamster bones as yet on the market. There are, however, some wonderful dog bones made of nylon. The bones have chicken bone meal impregnations which make them ideal for hamsters to use for keeping their incisors worn down. Nylabones are available at all pet shops. Photo courtesy of Nylabone Co.

hard objects on which to gnaw. If this is the case, the teeth do not wear down as they should. Poor feeding, especially of a breeding female and her offspring, may also result in the dentine, cement, and enamel being too soft. This too may create uneven wear.

If a pet does display malocclusion, the situation can be overcome by the vet trimming the teeth periodically; but clearly this is undesirable. This is why it is important to purchase only well-bred individuals. Problems with molars are seen less, because the movement of

the lower jaw usually allows for sufficient grinding of the teeth surfaces against each other, and against food.

HAMSTER CLASSIFICATION

The way all life organisms are formally classified by zoologists is very simple but can appear complex to the beginner. This is largely because Latin (with some Greek and other languages) is the basis of the system. Additionally, because there are about one million animal

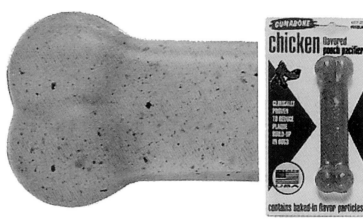

species, any system will have some complexity in its arrangement if it is to be a worthwhile means of identifying so many animals.

The common feature of all animals is that they are living, so all are placed in the kingdom Animalia. Plants have their own kingdom, but the same system is applied to them. The kingdom is divided into a number of groups called phyla (singular, phylum), based on given similarities between members. Each phylum is then divided, again using similarities as the point of reference. This creates a rank known as the class. Well-known examples of classes are birds (Aves),

reptiles (Reptilia), fish (Osteichthyes), insects (Insecta) and mammals (Mammalia). The classes are divided into orders, the orders into families, the families into genera, and the genera into species. Below the species there are subspecies, which are the lowest rank in formal animal classification. As you move down the ranks, the members share more and more features with each other.

The order Rodentia is divided into three suborders.

Sciuromorpha contains the beavers, squirrels, gophers, kangaroo and pocket mice. Hystricomorpha includes the porcupines, guinea pigs, coypu, chinchillas, and their like. The third suborder is the one of interest to us. It is Myomorpha, and houses the mice, rats, lemmings, voles, gerbils, and hamsters.

The myomorphs are divided into nine families. One of them is called Muridae. It contains about 1,139 species, so it is the largest rodent and mammalian family, comprising 25 percent of all mammals. The murids are divided into 16 subfamilies, the hamster being in that called Cricetinae. It contains

Long-haired hamsters don't exist in nature, but they are very wonderful pets.

just 6 genera and 20 or so species, authorities differing on the exact number recognized. The classification of the rodents has always been the subject of debate among zoologists, and remains so to this day.

A species is a group of animals that will breed quite naturally in the wild state and produce fertile offspring that resemble their parents. A subspecies is a group of individuals of a species that differ sufficiently, and constantly, to be accorded recognition as a group. Generally, they have been separated from the other members of their species by some physical barrier. With the passage of time, they may become distinct, and isolated, enough to be regarded as a full species.

A species is identified by giving it two names. One indicates its genus—the generic name. The other is the species, specific, or trivial name. The two used together uniquely identify it as a species. The generic part of the name always begins with a capital letter; the trivial name always begins with a lowercase letter. The scientific name is written in a typeface that differs from the main body of text. It is thus normally seen in italics.

Scientific names are international in use, whereas common names are not. The latter are not bound by any code of application. This means that a given species may have two or more common names, and confusion can often arise with respect to species being

A new color variety with a new personality. This specimen is not afraid of people; it eagerly greets visitors the way dogs do!

referred to. This cannot happen if the binomial system of nomenclature, as discussed here, is understood and used by hobbyists.

THE GOLDEN, OR SYRIAN, HAMSTER

The golden hamster is by far the most well-known cricetid, so its life style is discussed here.

Distribution: The golden hamster, *Mesocricetus auratus*, is native to the region of Aleppo in Syria. It has the smallest distribution range of any hamster. If, as some experts believe, the related species *M.brandti* is a subspecies of *auratus*, then the range of distribution is far more extensive, encompassing a large area of Asia Minor.

The golden hamster is additionally interesting in that its range is overlapped by two hamsters of different genera. Some experts believe that it is a hybrid of the two; others believe that one of the two is a subspecies of the golden, and has simply expanded its range.

Size: Head to tail length is about 17-18cm, the tail accounting for only about 1.2cm. The weight range is 97-113 grams in *auratus*, but up to 248 grams for *brandti*, making this a much stockier hamster.

A hamster is about 7 inches (17-18cm) long; the tail is only half an inch in length. They weigh between 3 and 4 ounces.

This is a golden satin hamster female.

Color: The upper parts of the body are a reddish brown with the belly, chest, and throat being cream or white. There are also dark brown/black bars that extend from the cheeks to the top of the shoulders. There may also be a black broken stripe down the back, so there is quite a range of markings within the species. The basic pattern of the red or golden color is agouti, in that the individual hairs are banded in red, yellow and black. But this pattern is less obvious than in the typical gray agouti pattern seen in mice, rats, rabbits and other species.

Lifestyle: Golden hamsters are solitary creatures that come together only to perpetuate the species. They live in burrows that contain toilet, nursery and food storage areas. Entrances may be oblique or vertical, often both being featured. The winter burrows may be considerably deeper than those used during the warmer months. The general terrain preferred by hamsters is that of dry loose soil on rocky steppes that may be arid or bushy.

Although basically nocturnal, hamsters may be partially crepuscular (dawn and dusk) and diurnal (daytime) in activity periods. During cold weather, they will retreat deep into their burrow and sleep for a period of a week or so before waking to eat from their cache. Then they will sleep again. They do not, therefore, hibernate over extended winter periods as do some other animals.

The wild diet appears to be omnivorous, comprising available grains, seed heads, assorted plant matter, insects, and possibly even carrion.

DOMESTIC HISTORY

Although golden hamsters were bred in England during the period 1880-1910, they apparently died out. Not until 1931 did more examples arrive in Britain and a few other countries. These specimens came from Jerusalem, where a breeding program had been established from individuals captured in Syria. Only one male survived to mate with two females. It is from this humble beginning that all domestic stocks were produced. The hamster arrived in the USA in 1938. A further infusion of wild-caught specimens was added to the gene pool in 1971, by which time this little rodent was already a very popular household pet. Since then, other species have also become established in captivity but as yet have not become as widely kept as the golden.

The first mutation in this species was the piebald in 1947. The ruby-eyed followed a year later. As the hamster became very popular, more mutants appeared. By recombination of the various mutations, the hobby now has an enviable selection of colors, patterns, and coat types from which to choose.

Hamsters were first introduced as pets into the British Isles about 1880. They were not very popular but found some use as laboratory animals. In 1931 they were re-popularized as pets, and this time they were popular enough to be the subject of hobby clubs.

ACCOMMODATIONS

There are a number of housing options for hamsters, depending on the cash available, the object of their being kept, and the personal preferences of the owner. Hamsters have, in fact, been given more consideration from commercial manufacturers than have other popular small rodents. The main features of hamster accommodations, which apply equally well to any other caged animal, are as follows:

1. It should be as spacious as possible. Apart from giving the pet more room in which to exercise, it provides you with greater opportunity to furnish it in an interesting manner. This in turn makes for a more interesting pet.

2. It should be sturdy in its design. The hamster is truly an expert at escaping any accommodations that provide the opportunity to do so. Wooden cages are easily gnawed by this little mammal, and it needs only a small hole for it to squeeze its lithe body through. Plastics that are not strong enough will also be gnawed—even thin aluminum has not always restricted this pet. Cage bars that are not neatly fitted into the base of the unit can be pushed by a hamster sufficiently that it can squeeze through them.

Given these facts, you should invest in a quality cage from your local pet shop, rather than think in terms of making your own unit. The quality of the cage should be such as to ensure it can be cleaned readily. Inexpensive cages will feature chromed bars that may soon tarnish and be a source of rust. This represents a health hazard. Likewise, poorly painted cages soon deteriorate and reveal the metal below, which will rust as a result of the pet's urine, or even regular cleaning.

Again, if you purchase a cage at the top end of the price range, it will prove to be the better investment in the long run.

HOUSING OPTIONS

There are three basic housing options from which you can choose. One is the traditional hamster cage. Another is the tube and drum system that represents an attempt to create a natural ecosystem for these pets. The third is an aquarium unit. The first named is the most

A mouse and a long-haired hamster get to know each other. Hamsters are twice as large and twice as heavy as the typical pet mouse.

restrictive in regard to the available size range; but if the pet is to be given plenty of exercise time outside of its cage, it is quite adequate as a little hamster home.

The tube system has unlimited expansion potential, but is rather costly. It is more labor intensive with regard to being cleaned thoroughly, and obese pets could get stuck in some of the tubes. Even so, it represents a major step forward in attempts to create expandable housing systems that take the natural lifestyles of a given pet into consideration.

The good-sized aquarium gives you plenty of scope to use your imagination in creating a miniature ecosystem. But, like the tube and drum system, large aquariums are rather costly. For the imaginative hobbyist, they are perhaps the best of the options if cost is not limited. As they were not designed for these pets, it is important that, for security, they are covered with a neatly fitting aquarium hood, or a sheet of weighted glass, plastic, or wire mesh. If glass or plastic is used, it should have numerous air holes drilled into it to allow for adequate ventilation.

Most pet owners will commence with a hamster cage, and may later progress to one of the two more expensive options. Breeders will use cages because such units can be stacked and moved around with greater ease than the alternatives. There is a wide range of breeding cages for hamsters. Such cages are smaller than those in which pets are normally housed.

HAMSTER HOME FURNISHINGS

Regardless of the housing style, all accommodations should contain certain basic furnishings. These will be somewhere for your pet to sleep, food and water receptacles, suitable floor covering, and accessories that will be exercise- or interest-orientated.

SLEEPING BOX

This may come with the cage, or you may have to purchase it separately. It needs to be large enough so that your pet can enter it without difficulty, but small enough to be cozy when filled with bedding material.

FOOD AND WATER CONTAINERS

Your pet shop carries a wide range of food and water containers. For food, the best

choice is a small heavy crockery pot, which is less easily tipped than those made of plastic. Crockery pots also have a long-wear life. Two will be required: one for dry foods and one for moist foods. Water may be supplied via the same open pots as just mentioned or by gravity-fed dispensers, which are clipped to the cage bars and prevent dust from entering the water. Buy the more expensive models as the cheaper types tend to drip. The nozzle should be metal; otherwise, it will soon be gnawed by your hamster.

FLOOR AND BEDDING MATERIAL

There are many materials that would seem suitable for covering your pet's cage floor. However, not all of these are as suitable as might be thought, so let us look at each of them.

SAWDUST. This is highly absorbent, so it is excellent for soaking up urine. The darker woods are less suitable because they will likely stain the coat of light-colored hamsters. The disadvantage of sawdust is that it clings to foods, especially moist ones such as fruit. Further, it may cause irritation to a hamster's eyes, as well as to the teats of female hamsters.

WOODSHAVINGS. This

Dominant spot female hamster.

material is less absorbent than sawdust but does not cling as badly to foods. It is less of an irritant. A deeper layer will be needed though.

GRANULATED PAPER. This commercially made covering has the advantage of being absorbent, yet does not cling to foods as much as the other materials. It is ideal for either the floor or bedding. Paper cut into strips also makes good bedding, as does shredded paper towels.

COMMERCIAL NESTING FIBER. Available at pet shops, this is an excellent choice for bedding.

SAND. This would seem to be a natural floor covering for hamsters, many of which live in arid terrains; but it is abrasive and will cling to foods. If damp, it will stain light-colored areas of fur.

SOIL. Garden soil is not recommended because it may carry the eggs of pathogens (disease-causing organisms).

PEAT. Commercial peat as a floor covering is fine initially, but it tends to become dusty as it dries and breaks up.

NATURAL PLANT LITTER FOR CATS. Relatively new on the market, this makes an excellent floor covering and is biodegradable. Regular cat litter is not, however, a good floor covering. It is too abrasive and dusty.

CAGE ACCESSORIES

The style of housing will dictate the number and type of accessories that you can feature. The tube system is the least flexible for accessories, while the large aquarium offers most scope. Some suggestions are as follows.

PLATFORM AND LADDER

Platforms are standard in some cages, or they can be purchased separately. They provide a place for the nesting box and increase the total floor space. Solid-rung ladders are best, but hamsters can cope with other styles as long as the angle is not too steep. Be sure the ladder is firmly fixed so that it does not topple over when the hamster is on it.

EXERCISE WHEEL

This may or may not be included with a cage. If you purchase one, be sure it is large enough for your hamster and is not the smaller model designed for mice. Once again, solid tread wheels are preferred to the open-rung types.

DECORATIONS

Natural or imitation rocks can add aesthetic appeal to your hamster cage, as well as provide greater interest for your pet. Those sold for aquariums are excellent. You can add novelty appeal to a cage or aquarium by including arches and other suitable ornaments designed for the aquarist. Apart from the many products you can find in your pet shop, you can also utilize a few items from your home. The cardboard rolls for toilet tissue and paper towels make nice tunnels for a hamster to explore. Of course, the hamster will soon destroy the cardboard, which can readily be replaced. Small twigs from fruit trees will be appreciated. They serve as good teeth cleaners for the hamster, help to keep the teeth at the correct length, and provide fiber, which is a good tonic for the digestive system. Wooden thread spools are another

item that will amuse a hamster—dangle one from the cage roof bars so that the pet can reach it.

LOCATION OF THE CAGE

Although hamsters can cope well enough with a range of temperatures, what they are less able to do is to adjust to rapid changes in heat levels. For this reason, never put the cage where it would be subject to the direct rays of the sun, or where cold drafts could cause rapid temperature fluctuations. Likewise, avoid placing the cage over any kind of heating unit, or where an air conditioner would constantly be blowing cold air on the cage.

If you have pets such as dogs or cats in the house, the cage should not be placed where they could intimidate the hamster by continually peering in at it. This creates stress, which is a major precursor of poor health.

ROUTINE CAGE CLEANING

Your hamster's cage should be routinely cleaned every week. The floor covering and bedding should be completely replaced at

Blond hamster male in an exercise wheel.

this time (not just covered with fresh material). Food and water pots should be cleaned on a daily basis, though water bottle dispensers may need cleaning twice a week. Be sure to clean the cage bars, because the hamster will probably rub its snout on them after feeding. This is a potential site for bacterial colonization that is often overlooked by pet owners. Be sure to clean well into the corners of the cage, as this is where parasites are often able to multiply unchecked. You

A perfect hamster home is set up inside a 10 gallon aquarium.

Hamsters and other pet rodents are not safe with cats around them. Sooner or later, the cat will kill the rodent. Keep your hamster safely locked in its cage.

A typical metal cage for hamsters.

can use household bleach for disinfecting the cage. Be sure to rinse the cage thoroughly so it does not contain potentially high levels of residual chemicals that might prove toxic to such a small animal.

All accessories should also be cleaned each week. Any furnishings that appear badly chewed are best discarded and replaced. Likewise, cracked or chipped food pots should be thrown away. For this reason, it is always prudent to keep spare pots so they are ready for immediate use.

If you have two or more pet hamsters, they should be kept in their own cages and not be interchanged. Likewise, if your pet should die, make sure that its cage is thoroughly disinfected before a replacement pet is accommodated in it.

Bear in mind that it is not easy to treat a sick hamster, which may quickly die if it contracts a major problem or disease. The best way to avoid this situation is to maintain a high standard in your cleaning routine—and of course by ensuring that the diet is well balanced.

Pet shops that sell hamsters also sell their accessories. Be sure to get everything you need for your new pet hamster at your first visit to your local pet shop.

A typical metal cage for hamsters.

SELECTION

Selecting one or more hamsters suited to your needs should not be something that is rushed. It is all too easy to purchase the first cute little hammy that is seen only to have regrets later. Although these pets are not expensive, this does not negate the importance of giving due thought to your objectives and the buying process. All too often, pets are purchased in haste, and problems start within days of taking the pet home. In some instances, the pet owner later sees desirable individuals that he likes better than his present pet.

IMPORTANT CONSIDERATIONS

Before selecting a hamster, the following are the things you should know about, or have given thought to.

1. How to recognize a healthy hamster, as well as one that is unwell.

2. The best age at which the hamster should be purchased.

3. The preferred sex.

4. The standard of quality needed.

5. Where to purchase the hamster.

The actual colors, patterns, and coat types are not, in and of themselves, important from a management viewpoint. But, of course, they may be a major consideration to you. We all have our personal likes and dislikes. The only way they are likely to affect the purchasing process is that some are more readily obtained than others. The rarer colors and patterns

will be more costly. You may have to be patient and wait a while longer before the right individual(s) is located.

RECOGNIZING HEALTHY STOCK

Before all else, the hamster you select must be healthy. If it

Hamsters have been cultivated in different colors and different coats, but their physical characteristics have not changed.

is not, your entire enjoyment of the pet will be spoiled from the outset. Before you even look at the stock in a serious manner, take a good look at the conditions under which it is living. The things you should be satisfied with are that the cages are not overcrowded, the floor covering is not unduly littered with fecal matter, there is food and clean water available to

the stock, and that the bars of the cages are clean.

The general cleanliness of the establishment should also meet with your own idea of what clean is all about. If a seller's premises are unclean and smelly, there is obviously a much greater chance that the stock could contract a problem via the parasites and bacteria that are likely to be resident there. The more hamsters that are on view, the more important it is that hygiene standards are of the highest order.

Satisfied on these matters, you can then concentrate on the stock. Being nocturnal animals, chances are the hamsters will be cuddled up together asleep, or in their nestbox. The seller will wake them, and you should watch to see that they are walking without any sign of difficulty, as with an injured leg. If one of them remains hunched up in a corner when all the others are up and running around, this is not a good sign.

It may be a rather shy individual, it may be feeling a little out of sorts at that time, but it may also be displaying the first signs of a more serious problem. If it is, chances are fair to good that the others have been exposed to the pathogens, even though they are presently showing no outward signs of a problem. If others in the establishment look as though they are not in the best of health, you should immediately leave. The longer you stay, the greater the chances you could become a means of transferring bacteria from one place to another.

If, however, all of the stock looks lively, you should next focus on the one or two individuals that have the most appeal to you. To assess good health the following are key points.

Dominant spot hamster female.

The eyes should be round and clear. They should not protrude unduly, nor should they be sunken. There should be no indication of staining of the fur around them, nor of the eye weeping.

The ears should be erect and totally free of any signs of wax, dirt or sores. Sometimes, a hamster may get bitten by a cagemate; a piece of ear may be missing or split. As long as this has clearly healed, it becomes a matter of personal preference as to whether or not that individual is purchased based on its other qualities. Keep in mind that such an animal would be unsuitable for showing.

The nose should be dry to just very slightly moist, but certainly not wet or showing signs of discharge. The nostrils should not appear swollen.

The fur should be stroked against its lie so that if parasites are present, they will be disturbed into movement. If fleas, lice, or mites are seen, this indicates unclean housing and general conditions. Check other stock to see if it is an isolated case, or if all the stock is infested. The skin should be totally free of lumps, swellings, abrasions and any kind of sores. There should be no areas of missing fur, nor should the coat lack "life." Dry fur and flaky skin indicate poor health and lack of balanced feeding.

The anal region must be dry and should show no evidence of staining or being wet. In hamsters, the disease known as wet tail is especially dangerous and highly infectious. It claims many thousands of these pets every year. It badly affects stock up to the age of eight weeks of age—which is the prime time these pets are sold.

The feet will typically have four digits on the front and five on the back. The hallux of the front feet is rudimentary or missing. Sometimes a claw can be damaged, or even lost, for any of numerous reasons. This will not affect the health of the pet, but all digits should be present on an exhibition animal.

THE BEST PURCHASE AGE

Hamsters are weaned from their mothers' milk as early as three weeks of age, so a pet can be purchased anytime after this. However, four to eight weeks of age is a better time to buy one. This is because the older youngster will have overcome the stress related to leaving its mother. It will be fully independent, having passed through the first difficult weeks of life. It will be stronger and more able to make the transition from its present home to yours with minimal problems.

Given the short life span of the hamster, two years being the average, you do not want one much older than six months of age. It is very difficult to assess age once the hamster has matured. Old individuals may start to lose their fur and are prone to benign tumors, but pet shops and breeders will normally be selling only young stock.

If you are planning to purchase breeding stock, it is perhaps best obtained when the youngsters are about three to four months old. By this age, they are pretty much fully mature; and you can see

You should only buy a tame hamster for a pet. Have the pet shop salesperson handle the hamster before you buy it!

just how good they really are. They will be ready to breed once they have had a week or so to settle to your routine. However, you should not think of breeding these pets until you have gained some practical experience in their management.

WHICH SEX?

It makes little difference which sex you purchase because both will make excellent pets. The male may have more odor associated with it due to its scent gland secretions; but if it is kept clean, this will not be a factor of any significance. The female is the larger of the two, but as there are large and small individuals in both sexes, this too is not a consideration.

Males will often start to fight once they are mature, and females may do likewise. If a male and female are kept together you will be presented with litter after litter of offspring. Further, the female may savagely attack her partner, so keep only one hamster per cage.

THE MATTER OF QUALITY

If you want a hamster simply as a pet, it is not important that it is an especially outstanding individual from a breeding or exhibition viewpoint. Your main considerations are that it is very healthy, young, and of the color or pattern you find most pleasing. On this latter point, do not allow yourself to be sold anything other than your favorite choice just because the seller does not have the one you want. By looking at a number of sources, you will eventually

find exactly the one for you and your family.

The potential exhibitor will, of course, need a hamster that displays excellent color and, in the marked varieties, a good pattern. This hamster will be a little harder to find and will be more expensive— the more so if it is one of the newer varieties, or a color pattern that is not easy to produce.

The potential breeder can trade off a little individual excellence in the stock purchased in return for proven breeding ability. An outstanding exhibition hamster may produce mediocre stock, so the would-be breeder must obtain individuals that are known to pass on their virtues. Clearly, an outstanding specimen that breeds as good as it looks is the most desirable choice, but breeders will tend to keep such a hamster for their own program.

WHERE TO PURCHASE YOUR HAMSTER

There really are only two

worthwhile sources of hamsters. One is the pet shop; the other is a well-established breeder. Never purchase these pets at flea markets or similar outlets. No credible or caring owner would even consider subjecting their stock to the conditions that prevail at such places. The risk of contracting disease is high, and the fluctuating temperatures can create considerable stress, as can the general noises that abound.

Retail stores may sell hamsters. In these instances, it is not that the pets lack care, or may be any more unhealthy than from a pet shop or breeder, but simply that they do not employ

Color varieties of hamsters are more expensive than normal colors, but if you only want a pet, buy the cheapest, healthiest hamster you can find!

trained staff who know anything about the pets they are selling. They cannot give you worthwhile advice, nor can they offer the standard of service and after-sales service of the pet shop. If you want a nice pet hamster, visit your local pet shop. You will also be able to buy *all* all of your pet supplies there. No other outlet can provide this sort of service. If you want show stock or a very rare variety, contact a breeder who specializes in such stock.

HANDLING HAMSTERS

If an animal has teeth, it can bite. This is as true of the hamster as of any other pet.

A friendly hamster with a mistress not afraid to handle it.

The young hamster that is well bred will be hand tame when you obtain it. However, the older youngster from an unknown source may not have been handled as often as it should have been. It is therefore prudent to approach an unknown pet with a degree of caution and respect. Although its teeth are small, a hamster can inflict a painful nip.

You can get some indication of the hamster's temperament by how it reacts to your approaching hand. If it sits on its haunches and grinds its teeth, this is a defensive posture, as is the individual that turns on its back. It is altogether better that you purchase only an individual that allows itself to be handled without fear biting. A typical youngster will allow you to slide your hand under its belly so its weight is supported. It can then be cupped in both hands, or stroked with the free hand if only one hand is used to lift it.

A less-than-friendly individual can be lifted using your thumb and index finger to grasp the loose skin behind its neck. Your free

You can get some idea of how tame the hamster is when it reacts to your hand in its cage. If it ignores your hand, bring it a little closer. But be careful...hamsters can bite!

hand should be used to support its rear end. Once on your palm, it is unlikely to bite. It will want to explore, when it can be gently stroked as part of its getting familiar with your scent. If you are very fearful of lifting the pet, a leather glove can be used initially just to lift it onto your free hand. It may bite the glove, but this will often be because you are applying too much pressure. After a few occasions, the time must come when you lift the hamster with an ungloved hand. Hopefully, it will by then have become accustomed to your scent and will not be as afraid as when it was first obtained.

Do understand that even a baby could nip. All youngsters "test" different surfaces as part of their learning process. Much depends on how gentle you are and, as already stated, whether the breeder handled the babies in the weeks prior to selling them. If you follow the advice given in this chapter, you will obtain a very nice hamster of the color and quality that you want. It will be healthy, easily handled, and a constant source of pleasure for the whole family.

Because your pet hamster will accept food from your hand, doesn't mean he won't bite the hand that feeds him! Be careful at all times!

Millions of hamsters are sold every year as pets for young children. The main reasons are they are cuddly, easily tamed, inexpensive to buy and feed, and very hardy if you take proper care of them.

FEEDING

Although the nutritional requirements of popular rodents such as mice and rats has been extensively studied and documented, that with respect to hamsters is rather less well understood, even though they are popular pets and laboratory animals. Be this as it may, enough is known to ensure that your pet can attain and maintain the highest level of good health.

The key to success in feeding these pets is a well-varied and balanced diet that will minimize the chance that an important ingredient is missing. The diet must contain all the important food groups in the amounts likely to be needed.

A properly fed hamster will be neither too thin nor too obese, will exhibit vitality, and will have a coat that reflects prime condition.

FOOD TYPES

Before looking at the constituent value of different foods, we should consider the various forms in which food is available. Basically it can be divided into three broad types.

1. **Dry Foods.** These foods have a relatively low moisture content. They include such items as cereal crops and their byproducts, seeds, and commercially dried foods such as fruits. Their advantage is that they store quite well, do not attract flies readily, and are not as badly affected by hot weather as are some other foods. They are the least expensive foods as a group and a valuable source of energy.

The foods in this group, which have a good shelf life, are commercially packaged as hamster food and sold in pet shops. Some pet shops will prepare and bag their own hamster mix.

2. **Freshfoods.** Within this group are all freshly cut plants, vegetables, and fruits, all of which have a high moisture content. Also included are foods that derive from animals, such as milk, cheese, yogurt, and eggs.

Their advantage is that they provide moisture, but more important is that they are often very rich in vitamins. Those of animal origin are rich in proteins and or fats.

Their disadvantage is that their feed "life" is the shortest of the three types. They are badly affected by hot weather, attracting flies and other unwanted organisms. Within a short period of time, they start to lose their nutritional value.

As they spoil, they can become the source of harmful bacteria.

3. **Pellet Foods.** These are technically dry foods because they contain little moisture. They are prepared according to various ingredient formulas. They are best regarded as a group unto themselves.

Their major advantage is that they are nutritionally complete. They are formulated to provide all the major

You can grow your own greens for your hamster. Pet shops sell greenhouse kits that produce everything you need for the fresh vegetables necessary in the hamster's diet. Photo courtesy of Four Paws.

ingredients that your pet needs. They are a very convenient form of food that, stored correctly, will have a good shelf life. They are not unduly attractive to flies and their kind, nor are they adversely affected by warm weather during the period they are likely to be left in front of a hamster.

THE PSYCHOLOGICAL FACTOR OF NUTRITION

We are constantly being told that this or that food is good for us, or for our pets. Food manufacturers will extol the virtues of "complete" diets, or of given packaged foods. The emphasis is always on the nutritional value to our physiological well-being—our metabolism. But what about the psychological importance of foods as part of the eating process?

Little is ever said about this because far less is known about it. What can be observed from your own eating habits is that if you lived on a diet of concentrated foods, chances are high that you would soon become irritable and unsatisfied, even though you knew your diet was technically "complete." The diet may well satisfy your metabolic needs, but clearly it is failing elsewhere. The end result is that you could become stressed, and this could adversely effect your metabolism.

The very act of looking over various food items, then taking the time needed to consume them, help to relax you. Eating is a natural part of any organism's social development. A complete diet food takes away your ability to be selective, which may well be for the good in some ways, but not in others. A hamster does not

Major manufacturers offer hamster diets without having done enough studies on the psychological factor of nutrition. Feed your hamster the same foods that your local pet shop used.

sit and reason things out as you can. In the absence of having a choice, it will eat what is there in order to survive. Its resulting mental state (stress level)

Hamsters of all color and coat varieties eat the same thing. This hamster is eating inside its feeding dish. BAD! It will soil the dish and ruin the food it contains.

rarely gets consideration.

This author has always held that no food can ever be complete. With this thought in mind, it would seem far better to keep the odds on your side and provide a diet that is drawn from all three food types. In this way, your hamster's metabolic and psychological needs will be fulfilled. You will be providing a wholly natural diet, while taking

Hamsters eat fruits, vegetables and seeds.

advantage of what science has been able to achieve via pellet and other complete diet foods.

FOOD CONSTITUENTS

Having considered the form of the foods that can be fed, we can now go deeper and see what constituents they must contain to ensure good health. Foods are comprised of proteins, fats, carbohydrates, vitamins, and minerals of various kinds, and in various quantities, one to the other. Additional to these elements, water is essential. The amount required in natural form will reflect the moisture content of the foods eaten. If the foods eaten are low in moisture, more water will be consumed. To ensure that your hamster stays in good water balance, it should have access to fresh water at all times.

CARBOHYDRATES. These comprise sugars, starches and cellulose in their various forms. They are oxidized during metabolism and release energy used by muscles for day-to-day activity. They also make some foods sweet, add bulk to the diet, and are utilized as food for certain bacteria in the intestines that themselves perform beneficial roles. They are required to aid in the correct assimilation of fats. They are the cheapest and most readily available food item. The richest sources of carbohydrates are cereal grains (wheat, rye, maize, rice), vegetables, and all plant matter. Certain carbohydrates are more beneficial than others, which is why it is sound policy to provide a range of foodstuffs.

PROTEINS. Without proteins,

Hamsters do get fat and overweight. If they remove food from the feeding dish and hide it in the cage, you are overfeeding them.

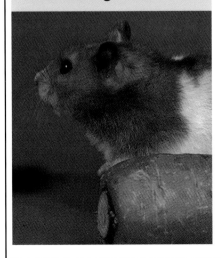

no organism could survive. The word itself comes from the Greek language—it means first place. Skin, hair, nails, eyes, muscles, blood and even those tiny units of coded information, genes, are made of protein. There are hundreds of different proteins made from chemical units called amino acids. Animals obtain their proteins from plants and from the flesh of other animals. These proteins are oxidized in the

Hamsters usually need water and a hamster water bottle is available at your local pet shop. If they are fed juicy foods (like ripe fruits) they might not need much water.

body and broken down to their constituent amino acids, which are then rebuilt into body tissue. For normal replacement of tissue lost in day-to-day wear and tear, hamsters need about 15 percent of their diet to be protein. But growing

No, the hamster is not praying! It is holding a seed while it removes the shell. They are cute animals, aren't they?

youngsters and nursing females may require as much as 25 percent. If this is not supplied, the result is a negative nitrogen balance (which is how protein is measured).

When this happens, the animal will break down its own body tissues to meet its needs. It will get thinner. The reverse is also the case; so an excess of protein will result in it being converted to fatty tissue, and the animal will become overweight. All foodstuffs contain proteins, but those such as meat and fish are prime sources. However, for the hamster, protein will be obtained in the form of plant matter, with perhaps the addition of some animal byproducts like cheese, milk, and similar items. Certain seeds, such as sunflower, peanut, most nuts, and soybean, are rich in protein and must be fed with care to avoid obesity.

FATS. These compounds give food its characteristic taste. Fats and fatty acids are essential to the body in utilizing proteins and carbohydrates efficiently. It is the richest source of readily available energy—twice that of proteins and carbohydrates. It is a rich source of the vitamins A, D, E and K. However, excess amounts of fat are harmful to the body, readily causing obesity and its negative side effects.

Fats are found in all foods but are especially associated with those rich in protein. Some foods, such as butter and lard, are virtually all fat. Fish and vegetable oils are other rich sources of fats.

VITAMINS. These are substances found in plant and animal tissue. Without vitamins, animals soon become ill and eventually die. Most are given letters to identify them, such as A,B,C,E and K, but they have names as well, such as ascorbic acid (vitamin C), thiamine (B1) and so on. Each vitamin plays its own role in the body, but it can also affect the other vitamins in a positive or negative way. The interaction of vitamins within themselves, and with minerals, is complex.

For this reason, the unqualified use of vitamin supplements is not without risk and should really be given only after veterinary consultation. Foods of plant origin are a rich source of vitamins, as are fish and other oils. Vitamins are easily destroyed or weakened when heated (boiling or other cooking processes). They are also negatively affected by exposure to direct sunlight.

MINERALS. These are elements in many forms. Examples are iron, copper, calcium, phosphorus, sodium, potassium and magnesium. They are essential to the metabolism of cells. Lack of certain minerals will result in poor health. But of the major components of food, minerals are the least likely to be deficient, though calcium may be a particular exception to this comment. It is the most-needed mineral, and it is vital to the development of good bone. This is why nursing female hamsters must receive ample calcium for the production of milk. From this brief overview of food constituents, certain facts emerge. Some foods are richer than others in given constituents. We cannot measure out the quantities of these constituents, even if we

knew what amounts were needed. The latter is dependent on many factors, such as ambient temperature, level of activity, age, health status, and other factors. All of this suggests that by supplying a varied diet, we minimize potential deficiencies. Finally, to gain maximum benefits from vitamins, remember that foods must be stored properly.

SUGGESTED FEEDING REGIMEN

The following items are but a few of those from which you can select. Dry foods can be purchased from your local pet shop, while freshfoods will mostly be those that you have in your kitchen. Wild plants can be gathered seasonally. Make sure that they, and indeed all freshfoods, are washed before they are fed. This removes any residual chemicals resulting from crop sprays. Avoid gathering wild plants from areas that may have been contaminated by car fumes or by domestic animals such as dogs or horses. If you have any doubts as to the identification of a wild plant (thus its possible toxicity), do not feed it to your pet.

DRY FOODS. The most popular cereal crops will be crushed oats or bran. Others that your pet will eat include wheat, rye, barley, and corn (maize). You can purchase

Fresh, leafy foods are appreciated by hamsters, but don't offer too much too often.

them by the pound and make your own mixture (including bird seed) if you are a breeder. But for the single pet owner, it is more convenient to purchase prepared bags of hamster food. This will contain a selection of cereal grains, rabbit pellets, and seeds such as sunflower. If you make up your own dry mixture, the following popular bird seeds can be included.

Canary and millet: These are rich in carbohydrates (58 to 66 percent), and low in protein and fat (respectively, 13 and 5 percent average). Millet on the ear (sprays) will be especially relished, either dry or after soaking in water for 12 hours.

Sunflower: The striped or white will be more favored than black. This is rich in fat (45 percent) as well as protein (20 percent). Carbohydrate is 21 percent. Linseed, safflower and peanut (unsalted) are comparable seeds. They should be given in limited amounts to avoid obesity. Pine nut is very rich in protein (30 percent) and fat (45 percent), low in carbohydrate (12 percent). Other seeds that can be tried in small amounts are hemp, niger, maw, rape and teasel. All of them are rich in protein and fat. Boiled rice may be appreciated from time to time. Dry whole-grain bread is excellent for the hamster's teeth, as are hard dog biscuits.

FRESHFOODS. Apple is one fruit you should feed. It appears to be especially valuable to breeding females. Most other fruits will also be enjoyed according to the individual palate. They include grape, cherry, orange, plum, strawberry, pineapple and others. They can be given fresh, dried or canned, though the latter have been sweetened, so feed with care. Bear in mind that your pet may prefer certain fruits to its regular dryfoods. It may gorge to the degree that it does not take enough of its staple diet items. Never supply so much freshfoods that they could upset the desired balance of diet.

Most popular vegetables will be appreciated. Examples are carrots (an excellent source of vitamin A), the green outer leaves of cabbage, peas, beans, beet (but this may stain light-colored individuals), celery, kale, cauliflower, lentils, soybean (very rich in protein and fat), spinach and tomato. It is best to cut all vegetables and fruits into small pieces and serve as a mixed salad, noting those which are ignored. It is always useful to know what foods are preferred so they can be used to tempt the unwell pet into eating.

Wild plants that are useful food items include hay (must be fresh and free of mold), dandelion, chickweed, plantain, and groundsel. Never feed any plant that has grown from a bulb, as it will be toxic.

ANIMAL DERIVATIVES. These foods can be used in moist or dry mashes, or fed on their own, depending on the individual item. Within this group are cheese, boiled egg,

Don't feed your hamster fried table scraps. This hamster is wisely refusing a fried potato. The hamster is a magnificent new black variety.

slivers of chicken, mincemeat, cod liver oil (just one to two drops each week on the seed or mash), and gravy stock. Feed these items only in small amounts. You can make a quantity of mash that will last for several days and store it in the refrigerator.

When making a moist mash, use porridge oats or bread crumbs as the base. Moisten with gravy stock or water, just enough to hold the constituents together. When feeding a mash, remove any that is left uneaten within two hours or so. You will learn what quantity of food your hamster needs on a trial-and-error basis. If a lot of food is left after a meal, you are feeding too much. If all is devoured, you are under feeding.

FOOD STORAGE AND HIBERNATION

Hamsters are hibernating animals in the wild, and this natural rhythm may occur with pets if the following conditions exist:

1. Deep litter that is infrequently cleaned.
2. The opportunity to store food caches.
3. Lack of regular handling.
4. Low ambient temperature—below about 58°F (14.5°C).

Avoid these conditions, and your pet will not become torpid. By weekly inspection of the nestbox, you can see if foods are being stored: they can be removed. Most hamsters will instinctively hoard *some* food, but it is when the other conditions, especially low temperature, exist that hibernation is likely. In the unlikely event that your pet did become torpid, you should place its cage in a warmer location, when the pet should slowly become active again.

Correct feeding is an acquired art that comes from observing your pet, knowing its likes and dislikes, supplying a varied diet, and ensuring that what is given is fresh, so that maximum nutritional value can be obtained. Follow these simple guidelines, and this will be one area of husbandry that will never be a problem.

BEFORE YOU BREED...

Before discussing the practical side of breeding hamsters, it is beneficial that you have some insight into the theory of the subject. To pair together just any available male and female hamster so that they can perpetuate the species hardly qualifies a person to claim he is a breeder in the true sense of the word. This type of reproduction requires no knowledge or forethought on the part of the owner, although this is the way many pet owners go about the business.

True breeders are hobbyists who carefully plan each mating with a specific objective in mind. They maintain detailed records that can be referred to when planning matings. These records are complete life histories and breeding histories of all the stock they own. By applying a planned system of matings and recording the results, a breeder is able to reduce the element of chance with respect to the outcome.

Of course, even the most carefully planned breeding programs can never completely overcome the chance element. This would assume the breeder knew *everything* about the genetic make-up of his stock, which can never be the case. However, the breeder can take measures to help reduce the element of chance in his breeding program: he can remove, or limit, the likelihood of faults appearing at every generation while increasing the possibility that desired features are retained and stabilized over any given number of generations. In short, his stock gets better because he is identifying and manipulating as many of the genes as he can.

A knowledge of genetics is by no means obligatory in order to be a top-class breeder, but it sure can help to minimize the number of wasted matings that might otherwise be undertaken. This is especially so when it comes to breeding for color or pattern. Genetic knowledge

can also enable you to avoid producing degenerate offspring, which would be the result if certain matings were undertaken. In this chapter, only the very rudiments of the subject can be discussed, but this may be sufficient to prompt you into reading more detailed genetic works.

HOW FEATURES ARE INHERITED

All features, such as color, pattern, size, length, head shape, many maladies, and even things like resistance to disease, temperament, and parental ability are passed from one generation to the next via units of coded information called genes. These are located on strands of tissue known as chromosomes, which are found in all bodily cells. It is not known how many genes there are on chromosomes, but the number of chromosomes is known for most animal and plant species.

In hamsters there are 44, which comprise 22 pairs. These are all virtually identical except for one pair that are

This mink hamster is, of course, a real hamster. It received the name mink *from the color and softness of its coat. It is shown here deciding which of the foods it likes best.*

found in reproductive cells and are known as sex chromosomes. They determine the sex of the offspring and may also control certain other features, including some colors.

The genes are arranged in a linear manner along the chromosomes, much in the manner of beads on a string. At each gene location, called a locus, there is a gene on the opposite chromosome of a pair that controls the same feature. The chromosome pairs separate when sex gametes are formed. Before so doing, however, they twist around each other. Some genes may move from one chromosome to the other, that from the other taking its place. They then separate, each chromosome forming a gamete—an egg or a sperm.

You can therefore see that each parent passes only one of its paired chromosomes to its offspring, the other coming from the other parent, thus restoring the paired chromosome situation in the offspring. If at every locus the genes on both chromosomes are the same, then obviously the offspring will look just like their parents. But if some of the genes on one chromosome are for a different expression to that of their opposite number on the other chromosome, matters start to change, and genetic knowledge starts to come into is own.

GENE ACTION
Some genes appear to be able to affect a feature when in single dose; others require

A normal golden hamster.

both genes of a pair to be of the same sort before they display themselves visually in the individual. Yet other genes work on a build-up basis. This means that a feature, for example, size, is not controlled by a single pair of genes, but by many pairs. For large size to be achieved, all the genes for that feature must be those for large size, the same being true for shortness. If an individual has some genes for tallness, but others for shortness, the

A light smoke pearl hamster.

resulting height will be somewhere between the two extremes. Such features are said to be polygenic in transmission, and most features are inherited in this manner.

We will focus on color because it is inherited in a more simple way, although it can still be complicated when numerous mutations are involved.

A cinnamon female hamster.

GENE MUTATION
Were it not for gene mutations, the subject of genetics would still be in the Dark Ages. It is only when genes mutate that they can be identified, thus studied in their mode of inheritance. A mutation is a change in the chemical structure of a gene such that it expresses itself in a manner different to the normal wild type gene at that locus. Its effect is to provide an alternative. Genes at a given locus can mutate a number of times. This means there can be a number of expressions at that locus. However, even if there are four or five alternate expressions resulting from numerous mutations, only two of them can ever appear in a single individual animal, one on each chromosome of a pair.

An example will make matters more clear, but there is another aspect that should be understood first. Genes have variable powers of expression. Some are said to be dominant, meaning they can display themselves when in single dose; others are recessive, and must be present in double dose before they are seen. Yet others are incompletely dominant and can make it appear that the genes were blending, which is never the case. Genes always retain their own identity.

There are also genes known as modifiers, which will change the expression of a feature between opposite extremes. For example, red can be intense or pale depending upon the number of modifying genes present. These genes are polygenic in action, but not like those for height. They modify the expression of a major gene, such as one for color, rather than create the expression of themselves, a subtle difference.

MUTATIONS IN ACTION

To illustrate a simple mutational action, we can pair an albino hamster with a normal golden hamster. In order to make calculations easy, geneticists use letters to represent the genes involved. Dominant genes are given a capital letter; recessive genes are given a lower-case letter. The letter used is based on the mutational gene locus. For example, one of the gene loci is known as the full-color locus. It allows all colors seen in the wild-type hamster to be expressed. One mutation at this locus resulted in no pigment being formed. This creates the albino (not a full albino in the case of the hamster, but we can forget this for our purposes).

The wild-type color is dominant to the mutational alternative, so it is given the letter C (full color), the albino being c (no color). Each of the parents has a gene at this locus on each of their paired chromosomes, so the full-colored parent has the genotype of CC, that of the

albino parent being cc. It does not matter which parent is which color because most colors are not influenced by parental sex. Where they are (as in the tortoiseshell), these colors are known as sex linked colors, and the sex must be considered when calculations are being made.

Returning to our example, you will remember that each parent can pass only one of its

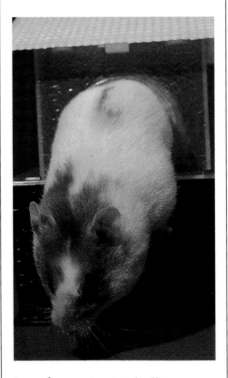

two chromosomes to its offspring, so each will donate one gene at each locus along its length. Which one is passed is a matter of random chance. In this instance, it matters not which chromosome is passed, because both carry the same sort of gene at the C locus. This means the offspring will inherit a C gene from one parent and a c gene from the other. Their genotype will thus be Cc. Because C is dominant to c, the youngsters will be normal golden in color—but

the recessive gene for albino is still there.

Such an individual is known as normal split for albino. This is written down as normal/albino. That before the line is visual; that behind it is the "masked" gene. From this example, you will appreciate that the same phenotype, in this case golden, may have more than one genotype. Indeed, there can be many different genotypes that all result in the same phenotype (visual appearance). Can you see the importance of a breeder knowing the genotype?

If you wanted to specialize in breeding normal golden hamsters, you would not want

A dominant spot female hamster.

one that had a genotype of Cc, for reasons we will shortly establish. You would want only CC stock. There is no visual difference between a CC or a Cc. Purchasing stock of unknown genotype would therefore be a waste of your money. If the individual is an outstanding specimen, you can remove the albino gene from your line, but this will entail breeding and selling stock that you need not have produced in the first place had you known the genotype.

In this example the only "hidden" gene is that for albino, but remember the normal golden could be carrying many hidden mutant genes at other color loci, which really would mess up your entire program. All sorts of unwanted colors or patterns could start to appear, and each would take time to remove by selective breeding.

CALCULATING A GIVEN PAIRING

The way you calculate what a given pairing will yield is by working out *every* potential permutation that could be produced. This does not tell you in all instances what any one litter will comprise, only what percentage chance you have of obtaining given offspring. In the case of the first example, you can be definite, because the permutation of CC x cc can only produce Cc, thus all the litter will be golden split for albino.

The method of calculation is to take the first gene and permute it with the genes of the other parent, then repeat for the second of the genes: CC x cc = Cc Cc Cc Cc = 100 percent Cc offspring. To complete the terminology you are learning, the CC and cc parents are said to be homozygous. They are purebreeding for the feature at that particular locus. The Cc offspring are said to be heterozygous, they are non-purebreeding for their genes at the C locus.

MATING THE HETEROZYGOUS OFFSPRING

If we mated two hamsters that both carried the genotype of Cc, we can now calculate what the theoretical expectations will be: Cc x Cc = CC Cc cC cc. There are 75 percent normal goldens and 25 percent albinos. Another way of looking at this mating is to say: There is a 1 in 4 chance of producing an albino; a 1 in 4 chance of producing pure normals; and a 50/50 chance of producing

normals split for albino.

If your objective was to breed only pure normal goldens, this mating would hardly be desirable! Statistically, your chances of *not* producing them is in fact 75 percent. The need to know the genotype of parental stock is thus very important; otherwise, a string of test matings will have to be undertaken just to establish what the parent's genotype is—a potentially long and costly process in some instances.

Another aspect that is often misunderstood is with respect to albinos. Although they display no color pigment, this does not mean they do not have any. If this was so, the mating just discussed could not produce 100 percent colored offspring. All of the pigments are within the albino, it being a case that the mutant gene, in double dose, prevents color pigments from being formed. In single dose it is ineffective, so colors and patterns are still created as in our example. When a gene prevents another from being expressed, it is said to be

epistatic. Thus albino is such a gene, because it has the power to mask all colors.

There are many mutations that are inherited in the simple manner discussed. They include brown, white banded, rust, and piebald, as well as the coat mutations of longhair, rex, and satin, although the latter mutation displays incomplete dominance.

PAIRING MUTATIONS AT DIFFERENT LOCI

If you wish to work out the results of pairing two mutations that are at different loci (in the first example the genes being considered were at the same locus), this is simple, but an extra consideration must be made that beginners

A blonde hamster male.

often overlook. Let us mate a longhaired hamster with another that has a rex coat. In both instances, the mutations are simple recessives in their action (they must be present in double dose to be seen visually). The result will be 100 percent normal-haired offspring. All will carry the genes for both longhair and rex in their genetic make-up.

The longhaired parent has the genotype of ll at the longhair locus, but we must consider its genotype at the rex locus as well. At this it is RxRx, representing normal fur, or non-rex. The rex has the formula of rxrx at the rex locus, but is LL (non-longhaired) at the longhair locus. The longhaired formula, or genotype, is thus llRxRx. The Rex is LLrxrx. We can now consider what each parent can pass to its offspring.

The longhaired can pass the genes l and Rx; the rex can pass L and rx. These are the only potential permutations. The offspring will have the genotype of LlRxrx. Rx is normal fur (non-rex) and is dominant to rex; LL is normal fur (non-longhaired) and is dominant to the longhaired mutation. We thus have all normal-furred hamsters, but they

carry the rex and longhair mutant genes in their makeup. They are normal split for rex and longhair, which can be written as normal/rex-longhair. The mutant genes cannot express themselves visually because they are in single dose. Always remember they are still present and could combine with the another "hidden" gene of their own type in another hamster, in which case a percentage of either rex or longhaired would be expected.

It would also be possible

for both of these mutations to appear in the same animal. Consider if the offspring produced from our last mating were paired. One of the 16 permutations would produce a hamster with the genotype of llrxrx—a longhaired rex! This individual would have long hair, but it would display some crinkles. The latter might not even be very apparent, so the double recessive mutation

created could easily be overlooked.

OTHER CONSIDERATIONS

From the foregoing discussion, it will be appreciated that much time could be lost in experimental breeding if you started out with stock of unknown genotype. It makes no sense, if you wish to take breeding seriously, to purchase hamsters from a "breeder" who has no idea of the genotype of his own hamsters. Of course, you can assess parts of a genotype

from the animal you're looking at. An albino is obviously cc at the C locus, but what is it masking at all the other loci? A dark gray hamster clearly has dgdg in its genotype, but it could be carrying a number of other recessive gene mutations in single dose.

If you have cute pet hamsters, but have decided to become a breeder, do not use your pets. Start with quality stock. This is more expensive, but it will definitely prove to be the much more prudent way to proceed. Why start with someone else's poor breeding stock? It will be easier to build from a quality base than to try and upgrade mediocre stock.

A lovely golden satin hamster.

Once you have the required hamsters of the colors or patterns you want, your next objective will possibly be to try and improve on them, as well as to improve or maintain the standard of conformation that exists. This can only be achieved if you restrict your breeding to hamsters that you know something about.

Just because a hamster looks good does not mean that it will breed to the same standard. It may have achieved its looks by the random chance permutation of genes inherited from each of its parents. These genes may

Cinnamon and golden hamsters meeting.

be in a very heterogeneous state, much as you now know colors can be. This being so, the hamster may be carrying a lot of faults hidden in its genotype. These faults may combine with the same faults that lay hidden in your stock. You may have chosen a particular hamster because it excelled in one feature, e.g., its head. But if it does not pass that excellence on, you will go backwards, rather than forward, in your breeding program.

So, it is not enough to select a hamster just because it looks good. You need to know that its good features are in a reasonably homogeneous state—so they will be passed on. Again, this is only possible if you can see a sampling of stock related to the one you want, and to know that the breeder has reached a given level of consistency by careful planning and record keeping. A breeding hamster known to pass on its looks, even if it is not outstanding, has greater value to the average breeder than a super specimen whose breeding is an unknown factor.

COPING WITH PROBLEMS

As you improve one feature another may regress: the color may lose some of its intensity, or the coat may lack the quality it formerly had in your stock. Breeding is full of frustrations and compromises, but the more you succeed the less you will use the services of a hamster about which you know nothing. You will be only too aware that years of hard work can be ruined in one generation by using a hamster of unknown breeding.

In order to overcome the problems related to inbreeding and linebreeding, both of which will be obligatory if you wish to become successful, your strategy should be to use outcross stock that is distantly related to your own. At the same time, you must test mate it to a number of your quality males or females, but keep the stock quite separate. This way, if results are not as hoped for over a few generations, your mainstream line is still untainted; and another individual can be sought.

Do bear in mind that when outside gene lines (bloodlines) are introduced, results may not always be overly impressive

It costs just as much to maintain a super show quality hamster as a pet quality hamster. But the youngster only cares about how friendly it is.

A black long-haired hamster.

in the first one or two generations. It can take a while for the desired results to be achieved. Many breeders discontinue using an introduced individual before its true worth has been established. The question becomes "Am I wasting my time with this hamster, or should I persevere a little longer?" That, I'm afraid, is what skilled breeding judgment is all about. All breeders are faced with such dilemmas, so you will not be alone.

There are numerous breeding strategies that can be found in books devoted exclusively to this subject. They will prove valuable to you. However, the best breeding practices in the world are of little use if the breeder does not select stock wisely. To do this, you must be able to recognize quality when you see it and be capable of casting a very critical eye on features so you can determine those in need of improvement.

Long-haired hamsters need regular grooming to keep them looking their best.

PRACTICAL BREEDING

Now that you have been introduced to the theory of genetics, you hopefully will have a general understanding of how features are passed from one generation to the next, and why it is important to begin only with quality stock. But there are other factors that you should know about before you decide to become a breeder. They are those related specifically to the process of reproduction, then the practical consequences of becoming a breeder. We will look at this latter aspect first. This chapter is written based on the golden, or Syrian, hamster. Much of its contents apply equally as well to other species.

THE COST OF BEING A BREEDER

All too often, beginners rush into breeding their pets without having made careful preparations beforehand. Nor do they consider the financial cost of the project if it is to be anything other than a one- or two-litter program. Even when hobbyists do make preparations for a breeding project, they are often wildly over opportunistic about the prices their surplus stock will command. Further, many simply do not appreciate that hamsters are not the easiest of pets to dispose of regardless of their selling price. The result of these realities is that many hobbyists become short-term breeders. They give up within a year or so when they find

that their great hopes did not materialize as had been thought. Their hobby has become a time-consuming and costly burden to them and interest is lost. Their stock is then sold at whatever price they can get. In so doing, they merely perpetuate the very situation that they no doubt complained about when they

were breeding—the low price of these pets in comparison to their upkeep costs.

A maxim that all breeders should hold as a golden philosophy is "prepare for the worst and hope for the best." By so doing, chances are that breeding will be carefully planned from every viewpoint. Frustration, which can never be avoided, will at least be minimized. As a breeder, the following are the costs that you must be prepared to outlay the minute you decide to breed hamsters.

You will need a number of

spare cages to accommodate the youngsters within a month of their birth. Extra food and water containers will also, of course, be needed.

Within a matter of months you will need a much larger facility to house all these cages than was originally the case. You will also need the space to store extra food

A cream satin long-haired male checking a black female prior to mating.

items, travel cages, and other items you are sure to gather as you progress further into the hobby. If an outdoor shed is purchased, it will need insulation and should be equipped with lighting, heating, and, ideally, water and a sink. Other accessories that will be beneficial once you are underway include: an ionizer to help keep the air clean, a thermostat for controlling the ambient temperature, and a rheostat so that the light can go on and off gradually, rather than suddenly via a standard switch.

Once the offspring are weaned, your feeding bill will start to go up considerably, as will the cost of cleaning materials, and all other things that were previously only minor-cost items when you simply kept a hamster as a pet. There is then the matter of finding homes for your surplus stock.

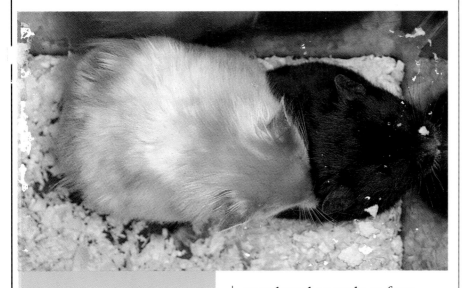

A black female and cream satin long-haired male mating.

If you are also interested in exhibiting, do not make the mistake of thinking that you will make a sizeable profit from your animals: Not all stock bred by exhibitors is of show quality. Additionally, don't forget the costs involved in exhibiting: travel expenses, entry fees, accommodations, etc.

All in all, unless you have a

rare variety, or species, you must regard hamster breeding very much as a hobby that you will have to support financially. If you expect to turn a profit, or break even, you will soon be disillusioned. The foregoing discussion has taken no account of the time you will need to devote to cleaning, planning matings, and so forth. Breeding is therefore very much a hobby pursuit suited only to the very dedicated enthusiast.

GETTING STARTED

Although the golden hamster may breed as early as four weeks of age, this is not recommended. The female will ideally be about 8-14 weeks of age, when she will be physically mature. She will peak in her breeding potential when she is about 10-15 months of age, after which time litter size will normally become smaller. Under no circumstances should you ever mate a hamster that is unwell, just recovering from an illness, or that has a weight problem. Each of these conditions will dramatically increase the possibility of birthing problems, or of the

offspring being sickly and lacking vigor.

Sexing hamsters is done by inspecting the underside of the anal region. The distance between the genitals and the anus is much longer in the male than in the female. The anal region in the male, when viewed in profile, tends to be more elongate than that of the female; but this is by no means a sure way to identify the sex of a hamster. The female may also be sexed at an early age by parting her underbelly fur, where her teats will be seen.

THE MATING

Mating in hamsters may be compared to that in many spiders in that it can be a hazardous affair for the male. A female not in estrus will attack her partner quite savagely. She might even kill him, so a high degree of caution must be exercised. Her estrus period lasts for about one day and occurs every four days. At such a time she will readily stand for the male with her tiny tail erected. Mating will take place very quickly if she is receptive. Evening is the best time to observe mating. This is when the female will be more receptive, being a nocturnal species.

You must be present at all times when matings are to be attempted. Place the female into the housing of the male, never the other way around. If aggression is observed, remove the female immediately and try the next evening, and so on until she is ready to accept her partner. Mating may be repeated over a short period of time. After about 30 minutes, you can remove the female and put her in her own cage.

Some breeders use "honeymoon" cages for breeding purposes. This is a neutral cage in which the male is placed first. Leave him there for about an hour and then remove him. His scent will have been deposited. Now place the female into the cage for a similar period, for the same reason. Next, place a partition—one made of stiff metal gauze works fine—in the center. Put a hamster on each

back into its own side and try the following day. It can be mentioned that hamsters of the opposite sex that have lived together since they were youngsters may mate and rear a litter of pups between them without the female ever getting very aggressive. However, you can never remove the male and reintroduce him at a later date—his former mate will probably not remember him. Even with a compatible

in milk. That which is left uneaten must be removed within a few hours so it does not sour.

BIRTH

The gestation period (time between mating and births) in the golden hamster is usually 16 days, but can be as long as 19. Never keep the female on a perforated or barred floor because this will invariably result in her destroying the

A honeymoon cage is one in which the male is placed in first to deposit his scent.

side of the partition so they can now see and smell each other.

Observe the attitude of the female. If she seems very interested in the male, the partition can be lifted and hopefully the mating will be effected. If she is clearly aggressive, put each animal

pair, there is still always the chance that a female may attack her mate. It is best to keep hamsters separated from one another.

THE PREGNANT FEMALE

If the female is already receiving a well-balanced diet, she will need no supplements, although some breeders feel that a little extra calcium in the diet may prove beneficial. You can either sprinkle powdered calcium onto her normal moist foods, or give her a small amount of bread soaked

litter. This is a possibility anyway, especially with a maiden female. Hamsters are very sensitive to their environment: any disturbance at birthing time (parturition) can result in the female practicing protective cannibalism. Keep this in mind and do not become overly inquisitive to look at the newborns. Otherwise, it may be the only sight of them you will ever get!

The litter range in this species is 1-16, but an average is likely to be 6-8. The young are born blind, naked and defenseless, but they grow at a remarkably fast rate. The fur is evident within a few days, and they are up and testing solid foods within ten days. They are weaned from their mother's milk by the age of 21 days. They should be removed from her within a week of weaning; otherwise, she may become aggressive towards them.

They can be handled once they are seven to ten days of

REARING

Once the babies are ready to leave the nest, it is important that the cage is kept as clean as possible. This is the time when wet tail, an especially dangerous disease, afflicts hamsters.

The youngsters should be handled more and more often as they approach weaning age and just after. This ensures they will be people friendly and ready to go to their new

takes place. Others play it by ear based on how well the youngsters are getting on together.

NUMBER OF MATINGS PER YEAR

In theory, a female can have nine or ten litters over a one-year period, but it is certainly not advised that you even attempt such numbers. The birthing process makes considerable demands on the

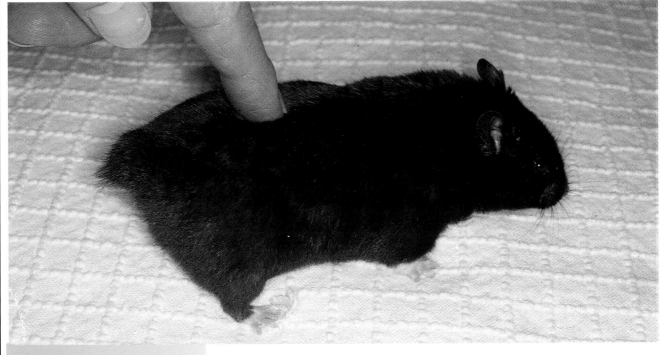

When the female is in season, even stroking her back with your finger will produce a mating stance.

age, but be sure to wash your hands before so doing. This has two advantages. First, you do not want to transfer germs to the babies. Second, if your hand carries the scent of food, a youngster just may try to bite your finger.

homes. They should be separated into same-sex groups once they are weaned, just to make sure there is no chance of an unwanted mating.

Once in same-sex groups, they are usually tolerant of each other for a few weeks, but then fighting may be observed. Once this is more than minor squabbling, remove the offender and continue with this practice until each has its own cage. Some breeders separate all youngsters at one time, regardless of whether fighting

female's body and energy. A mother hamster needs time to recoup after the pups are weaned. Four to five litters should be the upper limit—in the wild these little rodents have only two to three litters a year. They do not breed at all (in the wild) during the colder winter months.

RECORD KEEPING

No breeder of worth will produce offspring without keeping detailed records of all breeding activities. Without such records, it is not possible

Not every hamster color has an acceptable name. Many hamsters are named by local breeders so they can become famous for that particular color variety. The dealers, on the other hand, call them by more standard names.

to conduct anything but a hit and miss program. Your memory is very fallible; accurate records are not. They will be of tremendous value to you. Be assured that you will be consulting them time and again, the more so the larger your operation becomes. Just how detailed they will be is a matter of personal preference.

The following are some facts that you should record.

Name and number of each mated pair. Date of mating and date offspring were born (as near as you can determine). Number of offspring, their sexes and colors. If you are able to record the full or partial genotype for colors, patterns, and hair type, this is definitely

worth doing. If you are unsure of part of the genotype, use a dash. For example, a normal can be CC or Cc at the albino locus. The latter would be written as C- to indicate your uncertainty of the second gene.

Any that die should be recorded, as well as the reason

A large, but normal litter of 14 hamster babies!

for the death if this can be established. Any born with deformities must be recorded. It may be useful to weigh the youngsters at one week of age, and weekly after this. A drop in weight usually indicates a problem. All medical treatment given should be noted. Any changes from your normal feeding regimen (maybe you are testing a new food) should also be recorded.

Exhibition results can be written on this card, or they can be recorded on a separate register. Likewise, illnesses and treatments may be on a medi-

cal record attached to the individual's records.

ASSESSING YOUNG STOCK

It is never easy to assess the virtues of young animals of any species, and it is even more

You can't tell what color their coats will be until they get a lot older.

Three newborn hamsters on a $10 bill so you can appreciate how small they are!

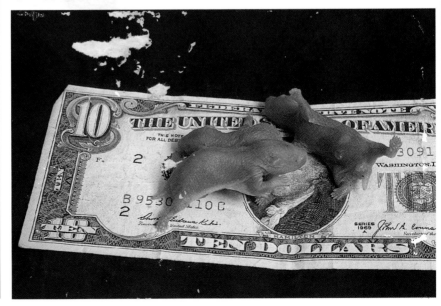

difficult if you are a beginner without the benefit of having seen very many examples. But you are going to have to make decisions about which hamsters will be kept and

As they grow up, their coat develops its color and texture.

which will go to new homes.

Try to see as many youngsters as you can in order to build up a mental picture of what excellent, average, and mediocre look like. Visiting shows will help you to learn what quality stock is all about. Talk to established exhibitors who can point out to you the major likely faults in conformation.

Hamsters will cohabit peacefully only while they are young.

There are various ways you can grade stock, either on a feature-by-feature basis, or by multiple scoring of a number of features, each placed in the order of importance to your needs. These systems of selection, and others, can be found in any good general book on genetics. The book does not have to be on hamsters—indeed, the chances are it won't be. Make the effort to study such works, and you will be well rewarded if you really wish to be a successful breeder.

The final advice to you in regard to breeding is that before all other features, health and breeding vigor should be given th

Yes, this was one litter. They are now ready to be sold; they must be separated or they will mate. Brother-to-sister matings are not ~~commended.~~

priority. Any female (or male) that produces sickly stock or that suggests fecundity is falling should be withdrawn from your program. Any females that cannibalize their litters for no apparent reason should not be ~~~~ the future.

One litter can have as many different colors and coats as there are individuals in the litter!

Do not lose sight of the fact that poor motherhood can be

EXHIBITION

It is true to say that the relative success of any pet, or group type, is a direct reflection on the exhibition organization that exists for that pet. The actual number of enthusiasts that compete in shows represents only a very small percent of the hobby, but that small percent is vital to the continuation and expansion of the hobby.

The hamster show is the shop window to the species, varieties and products that are available. At shows, you can see more colors and patterns than at any other single location. You can meet novice breeders and owners like yourself, as well as those with a lifetime of experience. For the serious breeder, the show is the only realistic place that the success or failure of a breeding program can be evaluated independently in a framework of competition against the stock of other breeders. In this chapter, space does not allow for details about shows, only a broad overview of the subject. If you are interested in becoming an exhibitor, you should visit shows and join your national hamster society. Have an experienced judge or breeder evaluate your stock so you do not waste time and money attempting to compete by exhibiting inferior hamsters.

A show-quality hamster will exhibit good conformation and color.

THE EXHIBITION HAMSTER

Hamsters are judged against written standards of excellence set by the national ruling body for these pets in a given country. The standard gives points to aspects of bodily conformation, as well as to color, pattern, and general condition of the exhibit. A total of 100 points is allocated, and points are deducted for faults. A good specimen will have sound conformation, display good density of color, and show quality of markings if they are a feature of the variety. The mutational coat forms will gain marks for the quality and texture of their coats. Apart from being an excellent example of its variety, a hamster must additionally be very friendly. No judge will take kindly to an exhibit that bites or attempts to. Such a hamster cannot be assessed properly, so it will have little chance of getting any award—if indeed it is judged at all. Clearly, the successful hamster will be well bred and easily handled, which means lots of training and/or actual competition experience. But these things alone do not ensure success. This comes from good day-to-day management. The best hamster in the world can be ruined if it is not fed and cared for correctly.

CLASSES

The size of the show will determine the number of classes scheduled. At major shows, all of the varieties will have classes, while the newer colors, patterns, and variants will be exhibited as Any Other Variety (AOV). There will be classes for males and females in each variety. There will also be pet classes for those owners who are not members of the ruling association, and whose hamsters may not be of top quality. Such hamsters are

Showing your hamster can be fun if it was a good quality to begin with.

GOLDEN HAMSTER VARIETIES

In looking at the color varieties of the golden hamster, I will also briefly discuss their mutational base. This information is presented so that breeders can be aware of those colors that are straightforward in their mode of inheritance, and those which can be more difficult to produce, or are associated with problems the breeder should be aware of. It is one thing to produce undesirable offspring in the light of not having information on known lethal and other genes (as when a mutant first appears), but to produce them when such data is well documented is inexcusable.

The prospective breeder should also be aware that a number of colors can be produced by different genetic pathways. Some of these are discussed. Likewise, some colors will breed true, meaning they are homozygous; others will not because they are only possible when in a heterozygous state.

GOLDEN

The original golden hamster still remains as popular as ever. It should be noted that the golden of exhibition standard is far removed from the wild-type golden, or even the average pet-quality

example. Its color is richer, and the markings are more obvious and striking. This is achieved by constant breeder selection for only the best-colored individuals.

CINNAMON

In this variety, the black of the normal (golden) is reduced to brown. The eyes are red, but they darken with age. However, they never become black, as they do in the golden. The color is inherited as a simple recessive. This means that a visual cinnamon is purebreeding for its color. It also means the color can be carried unseen in the genotype of a hamster. It is a very popular variety. As in all varieties, the color can vary in its depth and evenness. The underfur is brown, the skin bluish, and the underparts cream, as in the normal golden.

A normally colored golden hamster female.

Dark variants of the cinnamon are called rust. They are the result of a quite separate mutation, so they are not actually cinnamons. However, they could be mistaken for them, or even as being a light golden. The rust mutation is also inherited as a simple recessive. That they are separate mutations can be shown if examples of each are

A golden satin hamster.

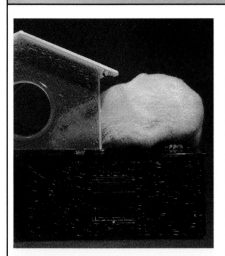

A blonde male hamster.

paired. The result will be a litter of 100 percent normal golden all carrying both the cinnamon and rust genes.

CREAM

There are many variations on the cream theme. They may be the result of differing gene mutations and combinations, or the result of breeder selection toward either extreme of natural variation within the mutation, or of modifier genes. All are very attractive. There is a black-eyed, a ruby-eyed, and a red-eyed. The cream is the result of a gene designated as e, which stands for extension series. This gene reduces all black pigment to cream of varying intensity. The cream is lighter in coloration than is the cinnamon. However, in the black-eyed cream, the gene does not affect eye pigmentation, nor the fur of the ears and genitals.

The red-eyed cream is the result of the cinnamon gene acting on eye pigment to reduce the color to red. It is thus a two-gene mutant variety, as is the ruby-eyed cream. However, this latter variety has problems in that the effect of the ruby gene is to make most mature males sterile. It also makes many females bad mothers. It is therefore not a popular variety any more.

Another cream is that created when the rust gene acts upon the cream to produce a darker-than-normal cream, but still with dark eyes.

BLOND

At the lightest end of the creams are the blonds, which are always very popular, especially with pet owners.

A pair of cinnamon, and golden satins.

They are produced by combining the light gray mutation, which is dominant, with rust, cream, or cinnamon. There are both black- and red-eyed blonds. The blonds are also called honey or ivory, depending on the shade.

ALBINO

There are no true albinos in the hamster at this time. But there is one mutant that is almost albino, and one that can be produced by a combination of two mutations.

A true albino has no melanin pigment, so it is pure white with red eyes. Its eye coloration is due to the hemoglobin in the eyes. The so-called albino hamster of the first type is one that is all white but has some pigment in the ears and genital area. Its eyes are pink, so it represents one stage up from true albinism.

Were it to carry pigment on the face and feet, it would be one stage up again and be called a Himalayan, as seen in rabbits, cats and other pets. The genes that create the dark-eared albino, Himalayan, Siamese, and similar patterns are all at the full-color locus. They can be arranged in a series going from the full-colored normal through to the full albino. A true example of the latter will no doubt arrive in due course, and it is perhaps surprising that one did not arise quite early in the development of hamsters as pets.

The second albino is created by combining the cinnamon mutation with the dark-eared albino. The cinnamon reduces the dark pigment to white or near white. These whites are very pleasing and should be pure white without any trace of

A black long-haired hamster.

Some color varieties are more difficult to produce than are others.

yellow, though this may be evident. However, the yellow may be the result of the environment rather than genetics. Urine staining will produce yellow, as will some types of sawdust when they are damp. Obesity may also tend to result in a yellow hue.

BLACK-EYED WHITE

There is no dominant white gene as yet in the hamster, but, as with the albino, a synthetic can be produced. If the white-bellied mutation is coupled with the cream, the

In hamsters, colors can vary in their depth and evenness of tone.

result is a dark-eyed white hamster of very attractive appearance. However, there is a down side to this pleasing color, but it can be avoided. The white-bellied gene is dominant, so it is evident when in single dose. This is as well because the homozygous form results in the eyeless white, or an individual with only rudimentary eyes. The healthy black-eyed white is therefore an obligate heterozygous carrying a single mutant gene, and a single normal (non white-bellied) gene. If two black-eyed whites are paired, the expectation will be: 25 percent black-eyed creams, 50 percent black-eyed whites (heterozygotes) and 25 percent eyeless whites (homozygous). The appearance of the eyeless whites is upsetting to breeders, so the color has never gained the popularity it possibly deserves. This is where genetic knowledge can be used to overcome the situation. If a black-eyed white is paired to a black-eyed cream, the result is 50 percent black-eyed creams, and 50 percent black-eyed whites. There is no loss in the potential number of white offspring, and there are no eyeless whites. Eyeless whites will be produced only if pet owners and uninformed breeders pair them together.

LIGHT GRAY

This variety is most attractive, being a light gray with just a small amount of light brown evident in the coat, mostly on the head. Here, the mutant gene works to increase the amount of dark melanin in what is normally yellow or brown in the hair shaft of the golden. The minor problem with this color variety is that

litter numbers may be smaller.

The reason for this is that the causal gene is a dominant lethal when in double dose. This means that all light grays are obligate heterozygotes. When two such hamsters are paired, the expectations would normally be 25 percent purebreeding light grays, 50 percent heterozygous light grays (light gray but carrying the gene for non-light gray (normal color)), and 25 percent normal golden hamsters.

The purebreeding light grays die prenatally, so litter size is

A light smoke pearl male hamster.

reduced. However, of the surviving offspring, you would have a 66 percent chance of light grays. The non-light grays (normals) have no light gray gene in them at all. If they did, it would be visible because the gene is dominant, so it could express itself in single-gene dose.

You can pair a light gray with a normal golden, and the expectations are 50 percent light grays and 50 percent normals, with a full litter size.

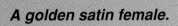

A golden satin female.

It is thus academic which route you choose. It should be mentioned that the single-dose light grays are as healthy as any other hamsters: there are no known negatives associated with the gene as long as it in single dose.

DARK GRAY

This variety appears somewhat like what you would expect a wild hamster with an agouti pattern to look like. The gold coloring of the wild type is replaced by a dark gray. The black flashes and the cream underbelly remain. It is a popular color. The variety may suffer from a minor problem that is not uncommon with mutations. There is a tendency toward smallness if dark grays are continually paired together, and motherhood may become questionable. The solution is to pair a dark gray to a normal that is known to carry the dark gray. The expectations will be 50 percent dark gray (homozygous) and 50 percent normal, but carrying the dark gray gene. From these results you may have correctly deduced that the gene is inherited in a simple recessive manner.

When the mutation is combined with cinnamon or rust, the result is lilac or dove. The lilac has red eyes and is a lighter shade than the dark-eyed dove. Both display a pinkish hue in their coloration. You will find that some color descriptions are not quite as striking on the animal as they sound by their name; the lilac and dove are possibly examples of such a situation.

PIEBALD

This very attractive color pattern was, in fact, the very first mutation to be recognized in the hamster. It is quite rare these days because it is associated with numerous problems. However, all breeders should be aware of the piebald because it is a classic example of how the white-spotted genes, which create various patterns, work. The pattern results in white and a varying amount of color. A piebald can be almost all one color, with just a small white spot, or it can be completely white with just a spot of color. The ideal is somewhere between the two extremes, often with a little more white than color. The spotting genes are unpredictable at the best of times, and are especially so in the piebald. This means that two apparently well-marked examples may produce a litter with only a few, or no, well-marked offspring, while a pair of seemingly poorly marked piebalds could produce a number of outstanding individuals.

This fact alone makes them a frustrating variety to work with and is why many breeders lost interest in them. When a breeder is reduced to pot luck over what is produced, he quickly changes to a variety where hard work and selection will yield its own reward. However, this is not the main reason why the variety lost followers after an initial flush of interest. It was found that piebalds were smaller than the average hamster. In addition, sterility in males was a problem, as was aggression. Further, it was also noticed that the number of surviving offspring in litters was lower than seen in other varieties. In other words, some babies were either dying prenatally, or just after birth, or were being cannibalized by the mother. This was especially noticeable when the matings were piebald to piebald for a number of generations.

Inbreeding depression, as it is called, was thus especially noticeable, and kicked in very quickly compared to what might normally be expected to be the case.

The mutant gene is inherited as a simple recessive, so it was thought that these problems might be overcome if piebalds were paired to normals split for piebald. This failed, as did pairing two split piebalds and accepting only a one-in-four chance of obtaining the variety. Clearly the problems are closely linked to the piebald mutation itself. Selecting only the largest and healthiest specimens failed to change matters, or rarely so. Faced with this situation and the arrival of the dominant spot mutation, the piebald lost enthusiasts. A few remain who are still attempting to separate the negative genes from those that control the actual color pattern.

DOMINANT SPOT

The dominant spot mutation was identified in 1964 and rapidly gained popularity over the piebald because its associated problems were much fewer. Like the light gray, the gene is inherited as a dominant that is lethal in its double (homozygous) form, so litter size is reduced. Although dominant spots are rather smaller than many other varieties, this is not always so; and they are invariably larger than piebalds. Mothering care is far better, so losses from litters are less, while the temperament of this variety is definitely superior.

In order to attain the required amount of white that is held to be ideal, only the best-marked examples should be used for breeding. Given the random nature of inheritance of this feature, this would seem a futile method. But it is still superior to making no selection for the pattern. Whether by luck or design, some breeders have been able to establish a relatively consistent degree of success, which suggests that some degree of control can be attained if one specializes in the variety and keeps very detailed records.

Even so, it must be said that any breeding involving the white spotting genes is best suited to those who have great patience and are prepared to accept a higher-than-normal level of failure in order to produce a few outstanding specimens. However, even poorly marked examples can be very attractive, so they have great appeal as pets—all is, therefore, not gloom and doom.

The two white spotted variants can be difficult to identify when a large piebald is seen alongside a typical dominant spot. Breeding behavior is the only 100 percent means of identification. If two "spotted" hamsters of unknown genotype are mated, you can draw a conclusion from the following: piebald x piebald = 100 percent piebald.

If any normal colored offspring are produced, then at least one of the parents (maybe both) is not a piebald. You must then conduct a series of test matings to establish which is which, or if both are dominant spots. This could be a costly undertaking. It would be better to seek out known examples of each variety, or the one required in the first place. It has to be added that the non-appearance of a normal does not conclusively establish

A dominant spot female hamster.

that you have piebalds, though it strongly suggests this. A repeat mating should be conclusive, based on the laws of chance.

If the dominant spot mutant is combined with the piebald, the result is a hamster with much white, with the color in small spots and blotches—almost in the manner of Dalmatian-type markings. In order to combine these mutants, you would need to pair a dominant spot with a piebald. This will produce dominant spotted offspring split for piebald. The other offspring of the litter will be normals split for piebald. If these dominant spotted are mated to their own genotype, you have a one-in-eight chance of obtaining a dominant spotted piebald.

The extent of white on either of these varieties can be increased by introducing the black-eyed white. However, you should be aware of the effects of this gene in double dose in order to avoid the eyeless white. Lack of this knowledge could result in the conclusion that the piebald or the dominant spot carried further disadvantages. This indeed happened, and the dominant spot gained an unfair reputation as a result. This underlines the need of those who breed these pets to have some understanding of genetics, so this kind of problem can be avoided.

BANDED PATTERN

This pattern is extremely attractive when well marked. Even poorly marked examples unsuited to the show bench can still be very appealing. Once again, it is a frustrating variety for the show exhibitor to undertake. Ideally, the band of white should be even around the hamster's body, and its line of demarcation from the colored fur should be straight and clean. Alas, this is rarely the case. The band may vary in width, may not encircle the body, and its edges may be very irregular and brindled. It is comparable to the Dutch pattern seen in rabbits, guinea pigs, and other pets.

The mutation is dominant in transmission, but in this mutant it is not lethal when homozygous. When it is combined with either dominant spot, piebald, or both, the white band is even more extensive.

All of the white spotted genes can be combined with colors to create an extensive range of combinations, because white spot is inherited totally independent of the colored areas. However, the theoretical dominant spotted cream is an exception: it results in a white, an example of how genes do not always interact as might be thought from calculated expectations.

TORTOISESHELL AND WHITE

This is a highly popular variety because it combines two colors and white. The tortie is also interesting because it is a sex-linked color. This means that the sex of the hamster will have a bearing on the color. All tortoiseshell hamsters will be females. A tortie and white can be seen in all popular colors (plus yellow and white). The mutation is not purebreeding, existing only in the form of a heterozygote.

The banded pattern has been utilized in the tortie to improve its color markings. The tortie is not an easy variety to breed to a high standard, because many of the tortie offspring will be poorly marked. Further, the possibilities from tortie matings is only 50 percent tortie, the remaining 50 percent being either yellow or normal coloration (normal meaning any of the other colors).

A magnificent black female hamster.

NEW COLORS

A number of new colors are being developed utilizing the umbrous or "sooty" gene that was first observed in 1975. This gene has the effect of darkening the golden color. In combination with cream, it results in a very dark brown, almost black, hamster. Other colors, such as chocolate, have been developed using the umbrous gene in combination with that for rust. A roan has been produced by combining the umbrous with cream and black-eyed white. However,

A cream long-haired satin banded male hamster.

you must always keep the latter in heterozygous form to prevent eyeless individuals from turning up in litters.

It can be assumed that in the future, new mutations and their recombination with those already existing will continue to provide the color breeder and the pet owner with a glorious array of colors and patterns that is sure to maintain the interest in this very popular little pet.

As it gets older, a black hamster may develop a brownish tinge in its coat.

COAT TYPES

There are now four choices to be had with respect to coat type. They are normal, satin, longhair, and rex. The normal is, of course, that displayed by the wild-type hamster.

Satin. This mutation, which is dominant in transmission, results in the hair carrying a super sheen to it. It also makes the color appear slightly darker, this being an optical illusion created by the structure of the hair follicle rather than by any change that has taken place in the actual pigmentation or its density.

A cinnamon satin female hamster.

It has been observed that when in homozygous form, the satin gene results in some loss of hair density. In order to avoid this, it is best to pair a satin with a normal, when you can expect equal numbers of satins and normals. The alternative of satin to satin is less desirable. Although your results will be three satins to one normal, the reality is that a third of the satins will be homozygous (ultra) satins and of little value to your breeding program. You thus end up with only the same number of quality satins.

Longhair (Angora, or Teddy). This mutation, which is recessive in its mode of transmission, is quite beautiful if seen on a quality male. The mutant gene is affected by male hormones. As these hormones are lacking in the female, her coat is far less impressive. The Angora coat takes a few months to fully mature. It is important to gently groom the coat as often as possible so that it does not become tangled or damaged by floor covering. Longhaired mutants are nearly always seen at their best on single-colored hamsters, rather than those that are patterned, whereby the long hair diminishes the visual effect of the pattern.

Rex. This mutation, which is recessive in transmission, results in a short plush coat. The coat's appearance is due to a shortening of the hairs, especially of the longer guard hairs. The whiskers are

They call this hamster a mink.

crinkled—one means of identifying this coat in very young stock. The rex coat as seen in the rabbit is truly magnificent, but this level of quality has not yet been achieved in the hamster and other pets that display evidence of the rex gene.

However, the early rex rabbits were rather bedraggled looking creatures with sparse coats. Only by very careful selection and breeding of only the very best can the rex in hamsters hope to become as outstanding as it is in rabbits. Selection is best made with youngsters, because mediocre youngsters may develop passable coats when fully mature. A youngster with a dense coat is the one to earmark for future breeding. This assumes it is a good healthy specimen in all other aspects. This is especially so of size, because there is a tendency for some mutations to stunt this feature somewhat, or to apparently do so. Unfortunately, mutations do not always appear in the most outstanding animals. The result is that in establishing a mutation, it is not difficult to establish the poor conformation of the individual that originally carried it.

Coat mutations are inherited independently of each other, and of color, so you can combine them in one individual. This may not always create a better looking hamster, although in the coat mutations discussed, they can do so if they are of very high quality.

A cream hamster enjoying his exercise wheel.

HEALTH CARE

The hamster is a hardy little rodent, and, given due attention to hygiene, feeding and general husbandry, it should live its life without any major problems. The single pet kept in the home is at much less risk to disease than is breeding stock, where large numbers may be housed in close proximity to each other. The breeder must be especially diligent in all aspects of preventive husbandry. Any lapse in attention to this could have catastrophic effects, as many breeders have discovered to their dismay. Being such a small pet, the hamster is not an easy patient to treat if it should become ill. Treatment may sometimes be as dangerous as the problem, or the problem may develop more rapidly than the treatment's capacity to stem it before the pet dies. Hamsters can easily become badly shocked or stressed if given injections, while oral administration of drugs is rarely easy with such a small creature.

Very often, a small pet may not display clinical signs of illness until it's at death's door, by which time medicines are too late to be effective. Diagnosis itself is not easy because certain diseases in these pets are complex and not fully understood. For all these reasons, it behooves the owner to concentrate on avoiding problems rather than treating them.

However, in spite of the rather gloomy prognosis just discussed, it is possible to treat unwell hamsters if the problem can be spotted in time for diagnosis and medicines to be given effectively. Much of what follows in this chapter is written for the breeder, but all owners should read the contents to see in what ways the matters discussed can be applied to their pets.

GENERAL HYGIENE

Your first, and most effective, line of defense against pathogens is always by routine hygiene. This prevents bacteria from mass colonization of the cage, food, or pet, and by so doing overwhelming the hamster's natural resistance to disease. Yet, time and again, owners will relax on cleaning chores. This is when pathogens take the opportunity to proliferate their numbers to dangerous levels.

It must be appreciated that many of the harmful bacteria are always present in the air. This means that they are not necessarily introduced by outside causes, such as infected newly acquired stock, tainted food, other pets, or even on the clothing of people, including the owner! A routine cleaning program should be as follows.

Daily. Wash each food and open water dish. Remove uneaten freshfoods, such as fruit, greens, vegetables and mashes not eaten within a few hours. Wash your own hands before and after handling your hamsters, and especially before and after handling unwell pets, or those suspected of being so. Breeders should sweep floors daily, mopping them if necessary.

Weekly. Completely clean, wash, and rinse the cage and its bars. Clean all cage furnishings and replace any that are clearly worn and cannot be scrupulously cleaned. Breeders should also disinfect floors and dust cage shelving each week.

The hamster(s) should be given a weekly physical check to see if it is in sound condition—much as you did when you purchased it. All foods must be stored where they cannot be tainted by mice, rats and insects. Nor should they be subjected to temperature fluctuations that might affect their nutrient value. A cool dark cupboard is the best place. Never let bags of soiled floor covering or any other trash accumulate in the breeding room. Dispose of them on a regular basis; otherwise, they will attract flies. Rapid temperature fluctuations in the home, and especially in the breeding room, must be avoided. Breeders should also be aware that a prime cause of health problems in a stock room is lack of adequate ventilation.

Whenever a number of hamsters are kept, it is wise to number the cages and all the food and water pots, as well as all furnishings. This way they can always be kept together. This reduces the possibility of pathogens being transferred from one cage to another during routine cleaning. It is also prudent for the breeder to have on hand a number of extra empty cages that can be cleaned and left empty for a period. They can then be used on a rotational basis.

The breeder should also consider at what point it would be wise to have a second breeding room. The temptation to continually increase the number of cages in a given space is ever present. If you limit the number of cages in a given breeding room, it will reduce the health risk that is always associated with keeping high numbers of stock within a single area of space. It limits the possibility that if a disease should be encountered, it will wipe out an entire stud.

QUARANTINE QUARTERS

The breeder/exhibitor is especially vulnerable to disease being introduced into a stock room via newly acquired stock, and by the people, many of whom are also hamster owners and breeders, that visit a successful stud. A quarantine facility is imperative. It need not be large—just a few cages. The most important factor is that it should be as far away from the main stock as possible. All newly acquired hamsters should be kept in isolation for about 21 days. During this time, their diet and health will be monitored. They will be carefully scrutinized for parasites, lesions and so on. A good magnifying glass will be useful to the breeder for this purpose.

When the isolation period is over, the newcomers can be introduced to the main breeding room. Put them at one end of the room and label the cages "new arrivals." Do not use them for breeding until at least another week

There are grooming tools specially designed for hamsters and other small animals. Regularly grooming your hamster will make him more friendly, more tame and more beautiful. Photo courtesy of Four Paws.

has passed. This gives them time to adjust to any local bacteria that may be in the breeding room. If they show signs of regression within that week, they can be removed promptly for further observation. The breeder who

spurns the concept of a carefully planned quarantine system is the one who may one day see his many years of hard work wiped out within a matter of a few weeks or less.

Every time a stranger enters a breeding room, he may introduce pathogens by means of his clothing. The conscientious breeder will take every step to see that his stock is not put at risk.

Always wear a nylon coat when attending your stock, as this material is less penetrable by parasites. Handle newly acquired and unwell stock with disposable surgical gloves.

It may sound as though you need a very sophisticated operation in order to protect your stock, but this is not the case, at least initially. The main thing is to spread your stock in the ways discussed and improvise the best you can as you steadily improve on each facility.

ENVIRONMENTAL FACTORS

The temperature, humidity, and light levels in a breeding room create the climate. The addition of noise and the presence of other animals, including humans, together with the contents and design of the housing, create the total environment in which the hamster lives. Any sudden changes or excesses in the environment can raise the risk of illness for various reasons. If a problem of any kind is encountered, whether on a regular basis or sporadically, it is always wise to review each element of the environment to at least consider to what degree it may have contributed to, or created, the problem at hand.

For example, it has been

established that the duration of light/dark periods (photoperiods) have a considerable influence on many breeding and behavioral traits. Further, if the artificial lighting used varies too much from that of natural sunlight, it may induce tumors. Manually operated light switches are more likely to result in photoperiod changes than timed automatic switches. Likewise, rheostat control of lighting (gradual on/off) is superior to simple automated switches. Time devoted to the study of these environmental factors could prove very beneficial to the breeder as part of his illness-prevention strategy.

Temperature fluctuations are always undesirable if they are relatively sudden. Apart from their own effect on the stock, they affect humidity. This can create problems if the temperature is too high or too low. High humidity levels, coupled with lack of adequate ventilation, together with fluctuating temperatures and uncontrolled lighting, represent a considerable spectrum of stress- and illness-inducing factors to a breeding room. They are additional to the general aspects of hygiene already discussed.

The pet owner's hamster is not at the same level of risk as is the stock of a hamster breeder. This is so simply because it is probably kept under conditions that are more spacious (the room it is in), more controlled, and in which there is not the high risk of illness that is ever present when a number of animals share the same confined environment.

WHAT TO DO IF YOU SUSPECT YOUR PET IS ILL

There is little doubt that many pets die each year because their owners either do not recognize that they are unwell, or they are too slow in reacting to obvious clinical signs. Clearly, if a pet displays no clinical symptoms and dies, there is nothing that can be done, other than to have your vet conduct an autopsy to see if the cause of death can be established. The pet owner may not regard this extra cost as worthwhile. A breeder should have this attended to because it may well prevent the loss of more stock. But very often the pet may indicate a problem by its behavior. It will show disinterest in its food, and may drink little, or more, water than usual. It may become reclusive when normally it would be in its exercise wheel, or scampering around its home. A friendly hamster may show signs of aggression that are quite untypical of its normal behavior, or it may be sensitive when touched on a certain part of its body. Each of these occurrences suggest that something is amiss and that some action must be taken.

The hamster's rapid metabolic rate is such that the hamster can quickly deteriorate if action is delayed for another day or two to see whether things improve—by then it may be too late. If you suspect an illness, you should do the following:

1. Isolate the hamster to minimize the risk of infection spreading to other hamsters or rodents that you may own.

2. Thoroughly clean out its cage, but retain a sample of fecal matter so that your vet can analyze it if required.

3. Place the cage in a warm location, which alone can do wonders for minor chills.

4. Make written notes of your reasons for suspecting the pet is ill. If clinical signs are evident, list them and try and remember when they were first noticed. How quickly have things deteriorated?

5. Now telephone the vet and give him all of the details of the situation. If he wants you to bring your pet into the office, be sure that it is protected from drafts, or a drop in temperature, when being transported.

If you are not able to contact a vet right away, try to regulate the cage temperature to approximately 80° F(26.7°C). This is somewhat higher than the upper limit temperature under normal living conditions. This may help to overcome minor chills or similar conditions. Temperatures any higher than this may induce stress that may aggravate matters in the absence of veterinary advice.

If the fecal matter is somewhat liquid, withhold greenfoods and other moist items, but do not withhold water. Periodically check the ambient cage temperature with a thermometer, which is always a useful item to have when small animals are owned. Be sure the cage does not get too hot if the heat source is not controlled by a thermostat.

PARASITE CONTROL

Domestic rodents are normally extremely clean animals. If cared for correctly, they should never become infested by mites, lice, fleas, and other similar parasites. Should these be visible, the housing must be cleaned immediately and treated, along with the pet, with a medication from your vet. A repeat treatment ten days later will be required to kill hatched eggs that were not destroyed in the first treatment.

Flies and other insects can be a problem, even in a well-run breeding room. Apart from being carriers of many dangerous pathogens, they are also intermediate hosts for certain tapeworms and pinworms. Anthelmintics in the feed will eradicate most worms, but control of the insects is the key to long-term prevention.

During the hot summer months when flies are particularly annoying, air conditioning or fans will help matters, as will old-fashioned sticky fly strips. Aerosols are not recommended because their continual use in a confined space may prove harmful to the hamsters. Dichlorvos strips used at ten-day intervals can be effective against mites and other tiny arthropods. Sustained use of these strips is not advised because of potential negative effects on the hamster.

Freshfoods must be removed within a short period of time, while all other foods should be stored in a way that prevents access by flies. Ultrasonic devices are also available to discourage insects, spiders, and their like.

MINOR CUTS AND ABRASIONS

Hamsters can sustain minor wounds from sharp objects. If bleeding is noticed, the wound should be cleaned with tepid water and a suitable antiseptic should be applied to prevent secondary bacterial invasion of the site. Secondary infection is always more dangerous than the wound itself. If a male is savagely attacked by his prospective mate and the injury looks bad, do not hesitate in getting the hamster to the vet. Keep it in isolation from the other stock until it has completely recovered.

DISEASES OF HAMSTERS

Hamsters can be afflicted with many diseases common to other rodents, such as mice and rats. However, the problem from an owner or breeder's viewpoint is that accurate identification can invariably be made only by autopsy after the pet has died. Even then there are problems, because the etiology of major diseases, such as wet tail, are not fully understood. Rather than being caused by a single organism, it appears that many such pathogens may contribute to the condition that is often regarded by breeders as a single disease.

As if this were not problem enough, the situation is compounded by the fact that hamsters are especially susceptible to the negative effects of antibiotics. Their use in treatments is thus risky and can prove as fatal as the disease being treated. The general prognosis when a major disease strikes a breeder's premises is not good. Often the stock is lost or humanely destroyed under

Observe your hamster constantly. If you see him lethargic, slow-moving, or injured in any way, isolate it from other pets and call a veterinarian or pet shop expert on hamsters.

veterinary advice. But in some instances, treatment may be worthwhile if particular hamsters are of great value. Attempts to save them have to be better than the unpalatable alternatives: doing nothing or destroying them.

Breeders must be especially aware of the seriousness of wet tail and what is known about it. The disease is scientifically known as proliferative ileitis, regional enteritis, or transmissible ileal hyperplasia. Clinical signs of the disease are dehydration, depression, anorexia, and diarrhea—the latter resulting in liquid staining around the tail and anus, a condition from which the common name is derived.

It is prevalent in weaning hamsters of three to eight weeks of age and can reach epidemic proportions in the breeding room once it has taken hold. After the first clinical signs are seen, death normally follows in two to seven days. The disease results in a thickening of the ileal wall; this creates stenosis (restriction) in the lower intestinal tract. A number of bacteria have been implicated in the disease, notably *Campylobacter jejuni* and *Escherichia coli*.

Tetracycline added to the drinking water for 10-15 days may be beneficial, as might kaolin-pectin given orally. (Check with your vet regarding dosage.) However, prevention

Note the difference in size between a Syrian hamster and a Russian dwarf hamster.

has to be the only realistic husbandry strategy. Stress appears to be a major contributory factor in bringing out what may well be a latent disease always waiting to happen if conditions favor it.

With this in mind, special care of the nursing female is a priority. Undue noise should be avoided, as should all other conditions known to be stressors. These conditions include overcrowding in a breeding room, uncontrolled and inadequate lighting, poor diet, parasitic invasion that upsets the female in her nestbox (mites and their like), and all climatic conditions that create an uncomfortable nursing situation for the female.

Keep in mind that if a hamster is already suffering from a problem, the problem can easily progress to a wet tail type condition if it is not arrested promptly. The distinction between wet tail and other intestinal problems resulting in diarrhea is not obvious, so never regard the symptoms as being some temporary minor condition.

USE OF ANTIBIOTICS

The reason that antibiotics are so potentially dangerous to hamsters (and guinea pigs in particular) is because they do not limit their action to attacking only pathogenic organisms. They will as readily kill microscopic organisms that are essential to the well-being of the hamster in respect to its ability to synthesize food, create vital vitamins, and aid the immune system. For this reason, the lay hobbyist should never consider administering antibiotics without the advice of a vet. To do so is to court disaster. Also keep in mind that the efficacy of antibiotics does have a definite time limit.

IN CONCLUSION

From this discussion, it should be appreciated that the identification and treatment of diseases in hamsters is not as easy as it is with larger pets such as dogs and cats. But it should not be thought that these pets easily become ill, because this is not the case. The vast majority of hamsters lead healthy lives, dying of old age rather than disease. The key to success lies with simple routine attention to their accommodations and diet.

OTHER HAMSTER SPECIES

Apart from the golden hamster, today there are others that are becoming established in captivity. This is to be expected, as there has been an upsurge in the keeping of "exotic" animals during the last decade or so. You should not be put off by the common names applied to some of these hamsters, such as ratlike and white-tailed rat, as these little rodents are every bit as much a hamster as the popular golden.

They will be more costly than the golden, and they do not as yet display anything like the golden's range of colors and pattern mutations. However, new colors are beginning to appear and more will follow. One tremendous advantage of some of these other hamsters is that they can be kept in pairs of either sex, or in colonies. (Just remember that in a colony situation, you have no control over which animals breed together.)

From the handling viewpoint, some are regarded as superior to the golden; others are not as good. However, during the course of captive breeding, tractability invariably gets better. Breeders will tend to select breeding pairs from those specimens that are the best for this characteristic. Further, it has been established that hormonal changes occur that, in many species, make the animals less stressed and excitable the longer the species is established under captive conditions.

DWARF HAMSTERS

Genus *Phodopus.* There are several species of dwarf hamsters. Although commonly called Russian dwarfs, one of the species, *P.roborovski,* has a distribution range that extends into northern China. The other two species are *P.sungorus* and *P. campbelli* of Kazakh, Mongolia, Siberia, and Manchuria. The last-named species is sometimes regarded as subspecific to *sungorus.*

A cinnamon Russian dwarf female hamster.

These hamsters are small and now quite popular. The color is a gray-brown above with white below. A black dorsal stripe, commencing on the crown, is seen in captive strains, but it may not always be as obvious in wild specimens. The lack of this stripe (partial or total) is a fault in British show specimens.

These species may live for just over three years. The gestation period is 18-19 days, sometimes a little longer. The litter range is one to nine, but four would be reasonably typical. The female has eight mammae. A satin mutation was identified in 1981 and is now well established. It is recessive in transmission. It may thin the coat, so only the best satin specimens should be bred. It also darkens the color, as it does in the golden.

In winter, a white coat is exhibited in *P. sungorus* in certain parts of its range. The normal coat becomes lighter as the daylight hours get shorter, and it may even become almost pure white. It can be compared to the situation seen in the Arctic fox (photoperiod and temperature), or in the Siamese pattern (temperature). However, you should understand that this is not a separate species, but merely a geographical adaptation induced by temperature and photoperiods. It can be induced in captivity, but an individual displaying such a phase cannot be entered into normal-coated exhibition classes. The species *P. roborovski* is very attractive, with large round eyes and longer legs than *sungorus.* Its ears are somewhat larger than in other species, and the natural coat length can be somewhat longer than that seen in other species. The dwarf hamsters are generally held to be the most docile species.

CHINESE HAMSTERS

Genus *Cricetulus.* In number of species, this is the largest hamster genus. The members are known as the ratlike hamsters because some do sport a quite long tail, and all of them have a longer body than other hamsters. The genus contains 12 species that are distributed from southern Europe to Siberia and China. Chinese hamsters were established as laboratory animals long before the golden hamster but were

A Chinese hamster compared with a Syrian hamster.

found to be less easily bred, so they were largely replaced by the golden when it appeared. At this time, the most popular species is *C. griseus,* which some authorities place in the genus *Cricetus.* It is entirely possible, given the overlapping range of some species in the genus, that present-day captive stock may actually be of different species, but are all regarded as *griseus.* The typical color is a gray-brown above with white or cream below. The feet and tail are white. The line of demarcation between the color and white should be as straight as possible. A black dorsal stripe is present.

The Chinese hamster will be in the size range of 7.6-10.2cm for exhibition

purposes (the largest genus member, *C.triton,* attains over twice this size). The body is long and, as in dwarf hamsters, the male will often be larger than the female.

The litter range is one to ten, with four to six being typical. Gestation period is typically 21 days, give or take 1 to 2 days depending on temperature and the individual female. The Chinese hamster is held to be somewhat more quarrelsome with its own kind, especially females; but this is diminishing as the species becomes more established.

About 1981 a black-eyed white spotted mutation was recorded in England. It is of dominant transmission. The extent of white seen on it

A Chinese spotted hamster, female.

follows the pattern of all spotted mutants in that it is extremely variable and not directly under breeder control. As in the golden hamster, it appears to stunt growth somewhat, but tractability is said to be excellent. Lack of fertility is, unfortunately, a problem.

WHITE-TAILED HAMSTER
Mystromys albicaudatus. This single species is normally called the white-tailed rat. It hails from South Africa. It is an unusual hamster in that it does not possess cheek pouches and has a very small litter size, typically three. There are four teats. The tail is long compared to many other hamsters. Color is typical hamster, being a gray-beige over cream or white. Ears are quite large, as are the eyes, this being very much a nocturnal species. Its lifespan of up to six years makes it very long lived for a cricetid.

COMMON HAMSTER
Cricetus cricetus. The largest of the hamster species, it is distributed from Europe to Siberia. It has never gained popularity in captivity, mainly because of its size and reported aggression. However, this may well change in the coming years due to its unusual color pattern.

The upper parts are shades of brown; but the underbelly, extending into the legs, is black. There are also white flashes on the throat that extend to the cheeks, on the shoulder, and at midriff level. These markings arguably make this animal the most striking of the hamsters. Albinos and pure blacks are known, so the species offers great scope for color breeders who may wish to tackle its questionable disposition.

It is a competent swimmer, inflating its cheek pouches with air. It is a ready breeder. Gestation is 18-20 days; litter size is 4-12, typically 6. The female has 8 mammae. However, its lifespan, which averages about two years of age, is rather short for its size. The common hamster is a solitary animal, but captive-bred individuals have reared young together. In the wild, the female will not tolerate the male after mating, so it would be wise to adopt the breeding strategy used for golden hamsters when breeding this species.

MOUSELIKE HAMSTER
Calomyscus bailwardi. Native to Afghanistan, Iran, Pakistan and parts of Turkey, this very small hamster sports a furry tipped tail as long as its body. The ears are very large, suggesting a desert habitat, which is the case. However, it also frequents grasslands. Its general appearance resembles that of a jerboa more than it does that of a hamster. Some zoologists believe it should not be regarded as a cricetid. Color is shades of brown above with white underparts and feet.

It is unlikely to ever become readily available in the near future because its status is questionable. In some parts of its range, it is regarded as common; in others, it is very rare and facing extinction. It is included here merely to complete this short overview of other hamster species.

INDEX

JONAS SALK SCHOOL
2950 HURLEY WAY
SACRAMENTO, CA 95864